Forbidden Places: 400 Facts from the World's Hidden & Mysterious Locations: Secret Bases to Sealed Archives— True Facts Behind Places You Can't Visit

Professor Poppy

Paperback ISBN: 978-1-997925-06-4

Electronic Book ISBN: 978-1-997925-07-1

Contents

1. Introduction

Within the world lie places shrouded in secrecy, mystery, and intrigue—sites guarded zealously by governments, veiled in legend, or lost to time.

This book unlocks the doors to 20 of the most fascinating, forbidden, and enigmatic locations on the planet. Each chapter presents 20 meticulously researched facts that peel back layers of history, conspiracy, science, and nature.

From the isolated tribe on North Sentinel Island to the classified high-tech base of Area 51; from the vaults of the Vatican Secret Archives to the eerie ruins of Italy's plague island, each page delivers insights that will intrigue, surprise, and educate.

This collection offers more than just facts. It invites you to explore the enduring allure of secrecy—how humanity protects, conceals, and sometimes unintentionally reveals its deepest secrets. Every chapter concludes with "Did You Know?" tidbits, providing memorable highlights and lesser-known curiosities.

Whether you're a casual reader captivated by hidden histories or a seeker of overlooked truths, this book offers an immersive journey into the world's best-kept secrets. Prepare to be enlightened, challenged, and captivated as you step behind the veils of secrecy that cloak these extraordinary places.

Welcome to a world less seen, full of untold stories waiting to be discovered.

2. North Sentinel Island — The Untouchable Tribe

Beyond the crashing waves of the Indian Ocean lies North Sentinel Island—an enigma wrapped in isolation, fiercely guarded by a tribe untouched by time. Attempts to reach or contact them have been met with fierce resistance, making this island one of the last great mysteries on Earth. What secrets does this hidden world hold? Journey into the unknown as we explore the astonishing truths behind the people who live beyond the reach of modern civilization, preserving a world many thought was lost forever.

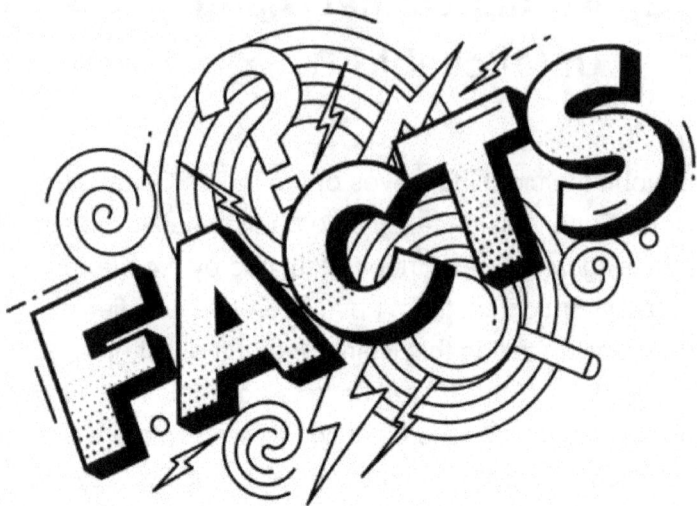

1. The Sentinelese are untouched by modern civilization.

The Sentinelese people of North Sentinel Island have had virtually no direct contact with outsiders. Their isolation is actively protected by Indian law, making them one of the last populations on Earth to live without influence from global society or contemporary technology.

2. Entry to North Sentinel Island is strictly prohibited.

Indian authorities prohibit visitors to the island under the Protection of Aboriginal Tribes Act, enforcing a buffer zone that makes landing illegal. Violators can face arrest or worse, as even well-intentioned trespassers have been met with hostility.

3. The Sentinelese communicate through unique language and gestures.

Little is known about their language, which appears unrelated to any spoken by neighboring tribes. Attempts at linguistic study have failed, as the Sentinelese are resolutely unwilling to interact with outsiders, making their dialect one of the world's great uncracked codes.

4. The tribe's population is estimated but never confirmed.

Estimates suggest there are between 50 and 200 Sentinelese living on the island, but nobody knows the exact numbers. Indian government studies rely on distant observations, aerial photos, and guesses based on visible encampments.

5. Outsider contact almost always leads to violence.

History records multiple tragic incidents when explorers, fishermen, or missionaries tried to approach the island. The Sentinelese use bows, arrows, and spears to repel intruders, prioritizing self-defense and seclusion over all else.

6. The Sentinelese survived the 2004 tsunami.

Remarkably, satellite images showed their dwellings intact just days after the disaster. Experts believe their environmental knowledge and vigilance helped them detect the danger, highlighting the tribe's resilience and deep connection to their land.

7. No outsider knows how the Sentinelese live day-to-day.

Since it's illegal and dangerous to approach North Sentinel, most details about their daily routines, customs, and beliefs remain a mystery. Anthropologists have only fleeting glimpses through encounters at the shore or aerial distant observations.

8. The Indian government chooses non-interference as official policy.

Recognizing the Sentinelese right to isolation, India has opted not to make forced contact, supply drops, or rescue attempts, even for shipwrecks near their shores. This approach respects the tribe's autonomy and protects them from disease.

9. The island's ecosystem remains nearly pristine.

Thanks to a lack of settlement and industry, North Sentinel Island's forested terrain and coastal waters are among the least disturbed environments in the Bay of Bengal. The Sentinelese reliance on natural resources reinforces their delicate ecological footprint.

10. The outside world's presence is mostly seen as a threat.

Historical efforts to "reach out" have led to tragedy. In 2018, an American missionary was killed while attempting to preach to the tribe—a stark reminder of the risks and ethical dilemmas involved in engaging with isolated indigenous groups.

11. The Sentinelese reject technological artifacts.

When outsiders have left gifts—coconuts, pots, or tools—they are often ignored or left behind. This aversion to foreign materials sets the Sentinelese apart from other Andaman tribes, which have sometimes adopted select technologies.

12. The island remains protected by law and nature.

Dense forests, shallow reefs, and rough seas are natural barriers that complement government policy, making North Sentinel both literally and legally inaccessible to nearly everyone.

13. Aerial observation is the only way to study North Sentinel Island.

Researchers use drones or distant surveillance to avoid disturbing the tribe. These efforts provide small glimpses of campsites, fires, and movements, but tell little about the deeper culture.

14. Their ancestry may stretch back 60,000 years.

Genetic studies of similar Andaman tribes suggest that the Sentinelese might represent one of humanity's oldest continuous cultures, giving the island immense anthropological significance.

15. The tribe's survival depends on rejecting outsiders.

Anthropologists believe past contact attempts led to fatalities not only from violence but also disease, as the Sentinelese lack immunity to common global pathogens. This reality underpins the strict non-interference still enforced today.

16. Indian Navy patrols the waters around North Sentinel.

Routine sweeps by the Navy and Coast Guard ensure no unauthorized boats approach, maintaining the legal exclusion zone and preventing both tourist curiosity and potential exploitation.

17. Local legends add layers to the island's mystery.

Neighboring islanders have long passed down stories about North Sentinel. Some describe it as cursed, haunted, or guarded by spirits—folklore that blends fact and fantasy due to the tribe's complete separation.

18. Wildlife thrives under Sentinelese stewardship.

Wild boar, birds, and marine life are all common near the island, partly because hunting and fishing practices are sustainable and untainted by commercial pressures.

19. The only documented peaceful contact was brief and cautious.

In the 1970s and 1990s, Indian officials left gifts from boats, including coconuts and cloth, which were accepted at times—but true dialogue or shared cultural exchange never occurred.

20. North Sentinel remains one of the world's last forbidden frontiers.

For global travelers and anthropologists alike, North Sentinel Island stands out as a symbol of ultimate isolation—an enduring testament to the human right to remain untouched and unknown.

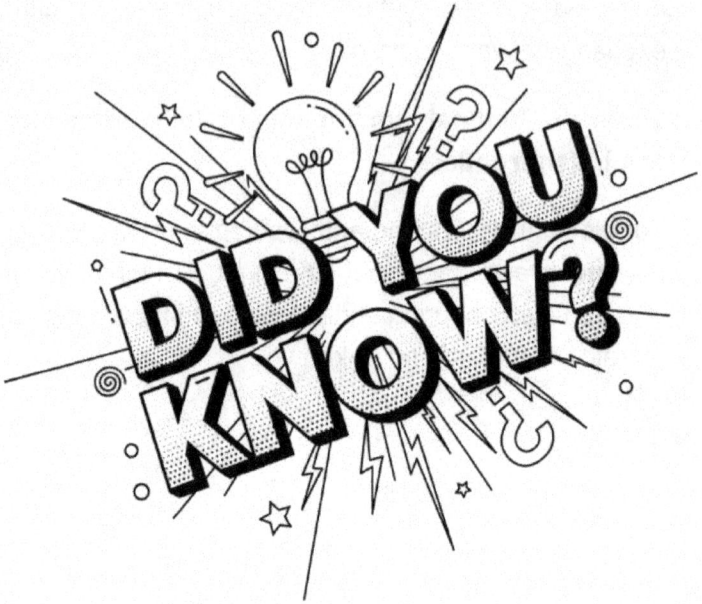

- Did you know the Sentinelese have successfully fended off every attempt at colonization, including by the British Empire, with none ever subduing or settling on their land?

- Did you know nobody outside the tribe knows what the Sentinelese call themselves, since their language remains entirely untranslated and unrecorded?

- Did you know the island's coral reefs create a natural defense, making it difficult for large boats to approach the shore safely, even in perfect weather?

- Did you know when aircraft have flown too low over North Sentinel, the tribe has been reported to shoot arrows and throw stones at the planes, signaling their wish to remain undisturbed?

- Did you know some scientists believe the Sentinelese may be direct descendants of the first humans to migrate from Africa, making their DNA and culture unique on Earth?

- Did you know after the 2004 tsunami, a government helicopter flew by with aid packages, but the islanders responded by firing arrows, making it clear they wanted no outside help?

- Did you know there are no clear photos of Sentinelese daily life or dwellings, since approaching with cameras could risk deadly conflict and violates Indian law?

- Did you know North Sentinel Island has inspired plotlines in novels, documentaries, and even adventure video games, but its true story is more enigmatic than any fiction?

3. Area 51 — Secrets of the Nevada Desert

Hidden deep in Nevada's desert, Area 51 is a place slipped beyond the veil of government secrecy and alien lore. For decades, whispers of experimental aircraft and extraterrestrial meetings have swirled, fueling endless speculation. Step inside this enigmatic stronghold and discover the truths and myths shrouded in dust and silence, where the line between reality and conspiracy blurs.

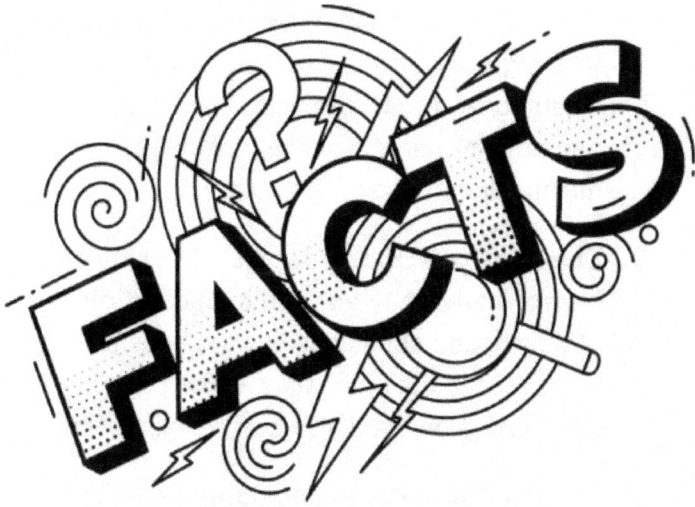

1. **Area 51's existence was officially acknowledged only in 2013.**
   For decades, the U.S. government denied its presence, fueling speculation and conspiracy theories. In 2013, the CIA declassified documents confirming the base primarily as a test site for spy planes and advanced aircraft.

2. **Established during the Cold War, Area 51 was central to aerial espionage efforts.**
   The base emerged in the 1950s as a secret site for testing the U-2 reconnaissance plane, allowing America to spy on Soviet missile sites without detection.

3. **The base spans a vast 23,000 acres of the Nevada desert.**
   Remote and naturally isolated, its size and location let the military conduct secretive flight experiments away from prying eyes.

4. **Area 51 is surrounded by restricted airspace and high-security measures.**
   Unauthorized flights are prohibited over the base, and armed guards patrol its perimeter, maintaining near-absolute secrecy.

5. **The infamous 'Storm Area 51' internet event humorously showed public fascination.**
   Millions joked about invading the base to 'see them aliens,' but authorities warned against trespassing on the highly secure military facility.

6. **The base was key in developing stealth technology.**
   Aircraft like the F-117 Nighthawk stealth fighter were secretly designed and tested here, pushing radar evasion capabilities to new heights.

7. **Employees at Area 51 operate under strict non-disclosure agreements.**
   Workers and contractors are bound by rigorous secrecy protocols, preventing leaks of classified projects.

8. **Satellite images reveal expansive facilities but little detail inside.**
   Though bases are visible from afar, details of daily operations remain hidden behind natural and electronic camouflage.

9. **The base's main runway sits on Groom Lake's dry lakebed.**
   Offering a natural flat surface, Groom Lake

facilitates testing of high-speed and experimental jets.

10. **Many UFO sightings around the nearby towns are attributed to secret aircraft flights.**
Unusual shapes and lights often attributed to alien activity have plausible explanations tied to experimental programs.

11. **Area 51 is believed to house underground facilities and tunnels.**
Speculation exists about subterranean labs and storage, though official confirmations are scarce.

12. **The base continues to test drones and cutting-edge unmanned aerial vehicles.**
Unmanned systems represent the future of warfare and intelligence, with trials held under tight security.

13. **Area 51 helped pioneer supersonic flight experiments.**
Many first-of-their-kind aircraft achieving high altitude and speed milestones were developed here.

14. **Despite rumors, no credible evidence links Area 51 to alien technology.**
Most UFO conspiracy theories remain unsubstantiated and are a mix of fact, fiction, and misinterpretation [mythical].

15. **The base has inspired countless films, TV shows, and novels.**

Its mystique underpins popular culture's fascination with government secrets and extraterrestrial visits.

16. **Local legends speak of mysterious lights and noises in the surrounding desert.**
These phenomena intrigue tourists and contribute to the base's lore.

17. **Personnel working at Area 51 are among the world's most vetted and secretive.**
Security clearance requirements ensure only trusted individuals gain access to classified zones.

18. **The U.S. government continues to invest in new technologies tested at Area 51.**
Research expands into cyber warfare, advanced avionics, and electronic surveillance systems.

19. **Area 51's perimeter includes decoys and disinformation campaigns.**
These tactics help confuse outsiders and preserve secrecy around actual projects.

20. **The base remains one of the world's best-kept secrets and largest black sites.**
Its function and scope continue to evolve as defense priorities and technologies change.

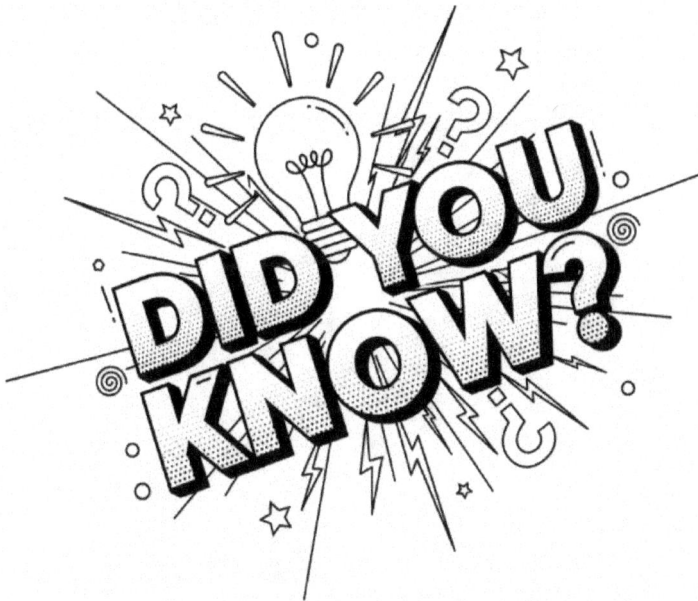

- The "Area 51" name comes from a 1950s map designation.

- The local town near the base, Rachel, Nevada, is known as the UFO capital.

- The base's runway can accommodate the longest and most secretive test flights.

- Early U-2 spy planes crashed repeatedly during Area 51 testing.

- The government has spent billions on maintaining Area 51's secrecy.

- Guards are authorized to use lethal force on trespassers.

- Some test flights occur under night-vision or blackout conditions.

- Area 51 has its own emergency medical and fire response teams.

4. The Vatican Secret Archives

Beneath the walls of the Vatican lies a labyrinthine repository of knowledge few dare to glimpse. The Vatican Secret Archives hold centuries of hidden documents, coded secrets, and untold power. What mysteries are locked behind these ancient doors? Enter a world where faith, history, and secrecy collide in a treasury of the unseen.

1. **The Vatican Secret Archives contain over 85 kilometers of shelving filled with priceless documents.**
   These archives safeguard centuries of papal correspondence, treaties, manuscripts, and state papers, offering a uniquely detailed window on church and world history.

2. **The word "Secret" indicates private, not hidden.**
   This term refers to the pope's personal archives, reserved for scholars and church officials, not secret conspiracies.

3. **Access is granted only to qualified scholars with special Vatican permission.**
   Application processes are rigorous, allowing only accredited historians and researchers to view specific documents.

4. **The archives include letters from Renaissance icons like Michelangelo and Galileo.**
   These documents reveal fascinating intersections of art, science, and religion.

5. **Many documents date back over 1,200 years, preserving early church history.**
   This vast collection includes papal bulls, medieval treaties, and other priceless manuscripts.

6. **The archives notably survived damage throughout wars and upheavals.**
   Their preservation speaks to their historical and cultural significance.

7. **Digitization efforts have begun but are limited due to fragility of materials.**
   Partial access to texts has increased, but most remain confined within secure vaults.

8. **Some files remain classified indefinitely for security and doctrinal reasons.**
   Controversial or sensitive materials are kept away from public scrutiny.

9. **The archives hold original trial documents from figures like Joan of Arc.**
   These records clarify the Vatican's role in major historical events and court proceedings.

10. **The collection includes diplomatic correspondence with European monarchs.**
    This highlights the Vatican's influence in global politics through history.

11. **Rumors of hidden prophecies and ancient UFO documents persist but lack verification.**
Such stories are largely speculative and part of popular myth[mythical].

12. **The archives store thousands of handwritten medieval manuscripts and illuminated texts.**
These are invaluable for studying religious practices, art, and literature of bygone eras.

13. **The archives are housed in a climate-controlled, underground section of the Vatican Palace.**
Advanced preservation techniques protect the fragile documents and rare artifacts.

14. **Some documents offer insight on inquisitions and church tribunals.**
They provide sobering evidence of the church's judicial history and moral complexities.

15. **The archives include early maps and charts revealing medieval geographic knowledge.**
These assist historians in understanding the evolution of medieval and Renaissance cartography.

16. **A small percentage of the archive has been made available to the public in exhibitions.**
Most material, however, remains under lock and key, accessible only to scholars.

17. **The archives' historical cataloguing system is still mostly unchanged since the**

Renaissance.
This continuity adds challenge and mystery to document retrieval and research.

18. **Some papal letters have shed light on church dealings during the Reformation.**
Correspondence reveals the church's strategies and reactions during religious upheaval.

19. **Church finances and state interactions from centuries past are detailed within.**
These files reveal the Vatican's economic power as well as its cultural influence.

20. **The Vatican Secret Archives remain one of the world's most prestigious and fascinating repositories.**
They are vital for understanding centuries of global history, religion, and diplomacy.

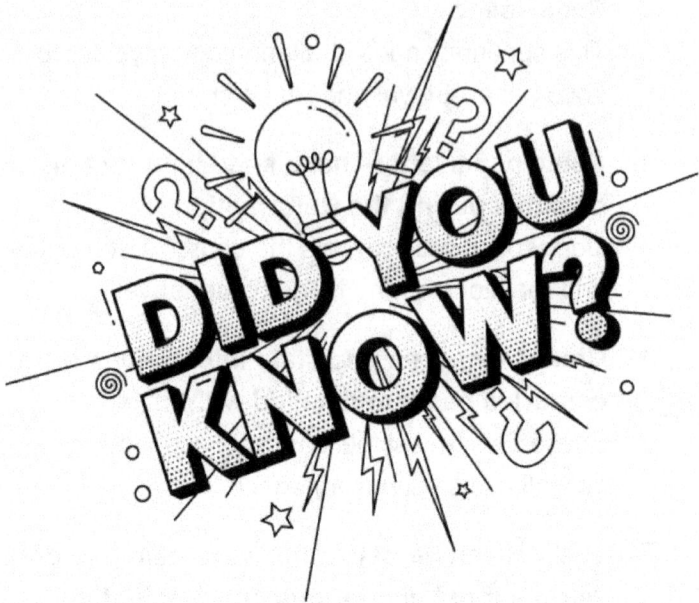

- The archives surpass 85 kilometers of shelf space, making them a vast historical trove.

- Studies show the archives have survived several fires, wars, and other disasters unscathed.

- The term "Secret" comes from Latin, meaning personal or private.

- Few people outside the Vatican have ever seen the majority of the documents.

- Some manuscripts date back to Pope Gregory the Great's era in the 6th century.

- The archives contain an original golden casket containing letters from Pope Leo XIII.

- Digitization began only in the 21st century due to concerns over document fragility.

- The archives once stored early works on alchemy and natural philosophy.

5. Poveglia Island — Italy's Plague Prison

Nestled quietly in the Venetian Lagoon, Poveglia Island carries a grim and haunting legacy as a place where plague victims were sent to die and tortured souls wandered its shores. Once a quarantine station and asylum, its abandoned buildings whisper dark tales of suffering and despair. Delve into the shadows of the "Island of Death" to uncover its morbid secrets and chilling past.

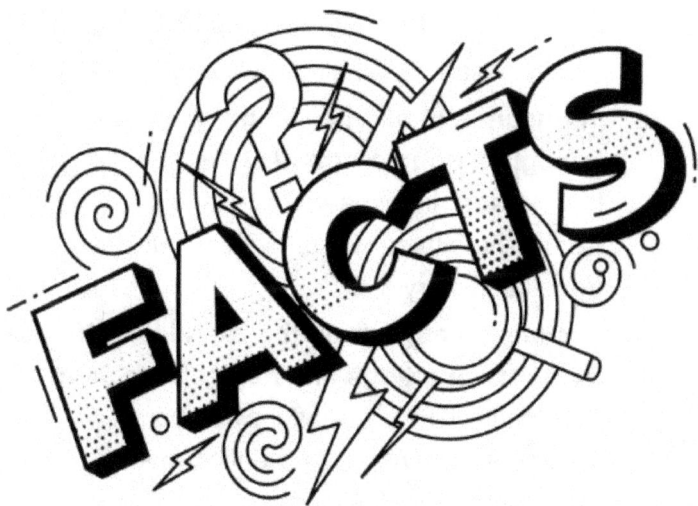

1. **Poveglia Island was a quarantine station used to isolate plague victims from Venice.**
   From the 18th century, this island served as a forced sanctuary to prevent the spread of deadly epidemics, where the afflicted were left to suffer in isolation.

2. **The island was later converted into a psychiatric hospital.**
   From the early 1900s until its closure in 1968, Poveglia housed mentally ill patients under grim and often brutal conditions.

3. **Today, Poveglia is off-limits by Italian law due to hazards and preservation concerns.**
   The island remains abandoned and inaccessible to the public, shrouded in rumors, decay, and historical silence.

4. **It is considered by some to be Italy's most haunted location.**
   Legends of tortured spirits and paranormal

activity have grown out of its tragic past though mostly based on folklore [mythical].

5. **Thousands of plague victims were sent to Poveglia during outbreaks.**
Mass graves lie beneath the island's soil, a silent testament to the devastating toll of disease in Venetian history.

6. **The mental asylum on the island is notorious for poor conditions and neglected patients.**
Reports from former staff include harsh treatments and neglect predating modern psychiatric care standards.

7. **Poveglia's decaying buildings remain a haunting visual for visitors on nearby waters.**
Ruined sanatorium halls and quarantine wards evoke a remnant of humanity's darkest medical struggles.

8. **Despite its eerie reputation, few verified hauntings exist.**
Most paranormal stories stem from its grim history and the psychological impact of abandoned ruins [mythical].

9. **The island's position in the Venetian Lagoon made it effectively isolated.**
This natural barrier made Poveglia ideal for disease containment but also contributed to its desolation.

10. **The asylum was shut down amid public outcry and changing mental health practices.**
Advances in psychiatry and exposure of mistreatment led to its eventual closure.

11. **Poveglia was briefly used as a military outpost during the 20th century.**
The island's strategic location was exploited by Italian forces during World War II.

12. **The island's name comes from a Venetian phrase referring to "small pond."**
It reflects its geography within the lagoon's intricate water network.

13. **Local fishermen often avoid nearing the island, adding to its mystique.**
Superstitions and caution persist among those who navigate the lagoon's waters.

14. **Archaeological studies continue to unearth graves and artifacts related to its infectious disease history.**
These findings provide insights into plague-era medical practices and quarantine rituals.

15. **The island's isolation served Venice well during Europe's periodic plague waves.**
Containing outbreaks helped maintain Venice's status as a trading and cultural hub during epidemics.

16. **While neglected, the island still hosts some robust natural flora and wildlife.**
Vegetation has reclaimed much of the once-barren quarantine grounds.

17. **The mental hospital buildings exhibit early 20th-century architectural styles.**
Despite ruin, their design reflects periods of institutional care development.

18. **Poveglia's bell tower is visible from much of the lagoon and serves as a somber landmark.**
It stands as a reminder of the island's laden history.

19. **Stories of lost souls and tragic deaths contribute to Poveglia's grim legend.**
These narratives, though speculative, perpetuate its dark aura [mythical].

20. **Today, Poveglia serves as an eerie symbol of isolation, human suffering, and public health history.**
It remains a solemn relic inspiring reflection on medical ethics, disease, and mental care evolution.

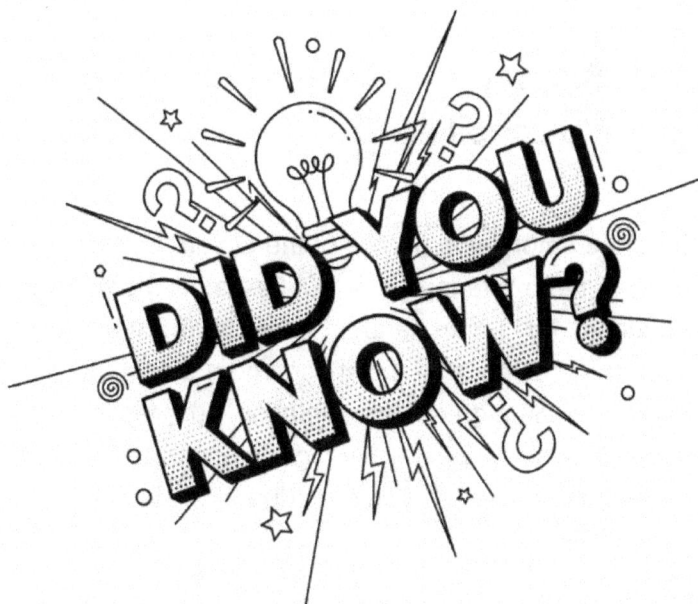
DID YOU KNOW?

- Poveglia quarantine protocols helped limit Venice's plague deaths.
- The island was officially closed to visitors in the 1970s.
- Mental asylum treatments included electroshock and isolation devices.
- The island was once used to bury bodies during the worst plague years.
- Paranormal investigators frequently visit illegally despite bans.
- The island inspired horror films and literature worldwide.
- Trees and plants now reclaim much of the decay and ruins.
- Poveglia's past reflects both medical advances and tragedies in Italy.

6. Surtsey — Iceland's Forbidden Volcano Island

From the unforgiving depths of the ocean, Surtsey erupted into existence in the 1960s—a newborn island untouched by human hands. Closed to all but a few scientists, it offers a rare glimpse into nature's raw power and the birth of life in isolation. Journey to this volcanic mystery, where every grain of ash tells a story of creation and survival on the edge of the world.

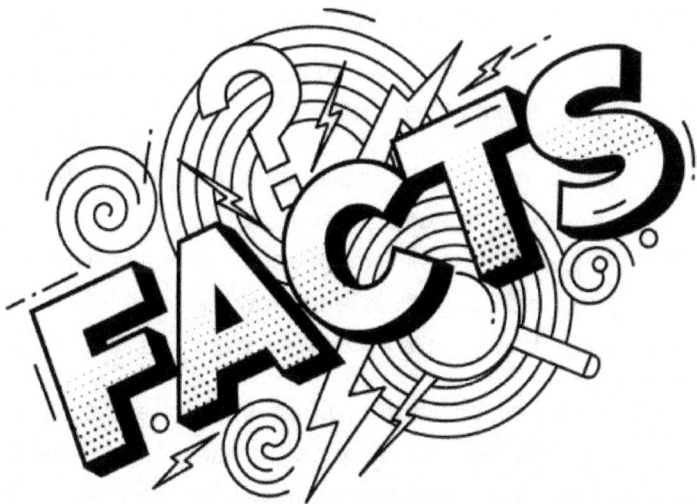

1. **Surtsey is one of the youngest islands on Earth, formed by a volcanic eruption in 1963.**
Emerging suddenly from the North Atlantic, it provides scientists with a rare natural laboratory to observe land formation and ecological succession from scratch.

2. **The island's name derives from Surtr, a mythical fire giant in Norse legends.**
This fitting name honors the fiery volcanic forces that created the island in a dramatic four-year eruption.

3. **Access to Surtsey is strictly limited to scientific researchers.**
To preserve its pristine environment, tourists and the general public are prohibited from visiting, ensuring minimal human impact.

4. **The eruption that formed Surtsey lasted from 1963 to 1967.**

This prolonged activity produced unique lava formations and created roughly 2.7 square kilometers of new land.

5. **Surtsey offers unparalleled insight into how ecosystems evolve on new land.**
   By studying plant and animal colonization over decades, scientists learn how life begins and adapts in hostile environments.

6. **Early colonization began with lichens and mosses gradually accumulating organic soil.**
   This paved the way for more complex plants and animals to establish themselves on the island.

7. **Seabirds, like puffins and Arctic terns, quickly made the island a breeding ground.**
   Bird guano enriches the soil, accelerating the development of a viable ecosystem.

8. **The island's volcanic ash cooled into black sand and rocky lava fields.**
   These geological formations create diverse habitats for pioneering species.

9. **Surtsey's formation is one of the best-documented volcanic events of the 20th century.**
   Volcanologists observed and recorded eruptions closely, providing vast scientific data.

10. **The island is still eroding and changing shape due to ocean currents and weather.**
    Ongoing geological processes reshape the landscape yearly.

11. **Strict protocols exist to prevent the introduction of non-native species.**
Scientists sanitize equipment and clothing to preserve the island's ecological purity.

12. **Surtsey serves as a model for understanding island biogeography worldwide.**
Its clear natural succession patterns aid conservationists and ecologists globally.

13. **The island shows how life can establish quickly despite harsh, barren conditions.**
Insects, birds, and plants have appeared in surprising rapidity since the island's birth.

14. **Surtsey's environment remains largely untouched by human interference.**
Its protection status as a UN World Heritage Site ensures this continues.

15. **The island supports species uniquely adapted to raw volcanic substrate.**
Pioneer organisms have specialized traits allowing survival in extreme habitats.

16. **The island has no permanent human settlements and is visited only for studies.**
Visits are carefully regulated to avoid disrupting the natural experiment.

17. **Surtsey provides comparisons to life on other newly formed volcanic islands.**
Its scientific insights help study similar remote environments and potentially extraterrestrial life forms.

18. **The island's black volcanic rock contrasts with Iceland's icy landscape, illustrating geodiversity.**
It's a vivid symbol of constant geological change in Iceland's dynamic environment.

19. **Lava tubes and caves formed during the eruption are key research sites.**
These unique structures preserve geological history and microhabitats.

20. **Many new species recorded on Surtsey later colonized nearby islands as well.**
The island acts as a stepping stone for ecological expansion in the region.

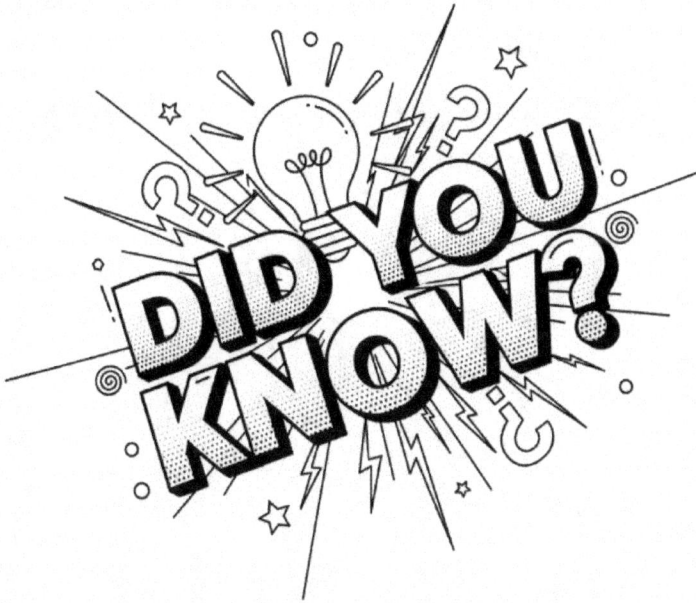
DID YOU KNOW?

- Surtsey is the youngest UNESCO World Heritage Site on Earth.

- The island's formation was visible from ships and airplanes in real time.

- Over 60 plant species have been identified since its creation.

- Seabirds returning to Surtsey bring seeds that help plant growth.

- No non-native species have successfully colonized the island.

- The island helped confirm theories of island ecology proposed in the 1960s.

- Scientists track volcanic gas emissions remotely to monitor changes.

- Surtsey is used as a reference for restoration ecology projects worldwide.

7. Fort Knox — America's Untouchable Vault

Wrapped in layers of steel, concrete, and myth, Fort Knox stands as America's fortress of secrets, housing treasures worth billions. Shielded by relentless security and whispers, it's a symbol of unyielding protection and mystery. Peer inside this fortress as we uncover the facts behind the legends and the ironclad truth of the vault that never opens.

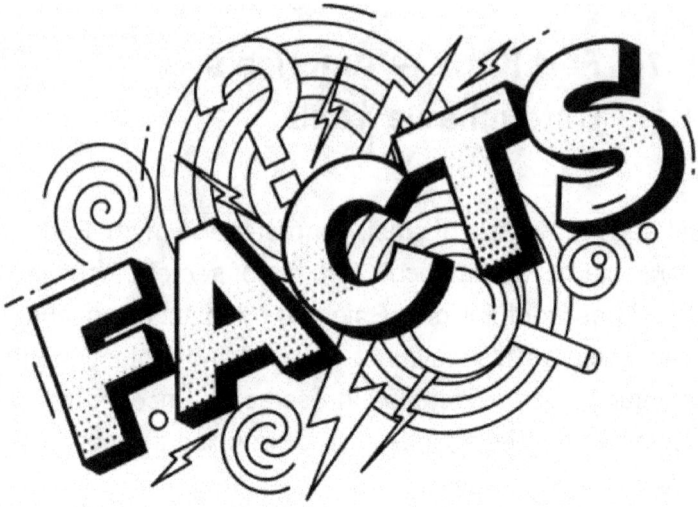

1. **Fort Knox holds the largest portion of the U.S. gold reserves.**
   With over 147 million troy ounces of gold bullion stored (estimated), it represents nearly half of America's official gold stockpile.

2. **The vault was completed in 1936 as a response to bank robberies and economic uncertainty.**
   It was designed to serve as the ultimate safeguard for America's financial assets during the Great Depression.

3. **The vault door weighs an astonishing 20 tons.**
   Its massive steel door combines state-of-the-art security and mechanical complexity to prevent unauthorized access.

4. **Fort Knox is located on a U.S. Army base in Kentucky.**

The military manages security, ensuring the fortress-like facility remains impregnable.

5. **Gold bars inside the vault are stacked on pallets, weighing around 27,000 tons collectively.**
   Each bar typically weighs around 400 troy ounces with serial numbers stamped for identification.

6. **Entrance is highly restricted and guarded by military personnel 24/7.**
   Only a limited number of trusted staff can enter the vault under stringent protocols.

7. **The vault's structure includes reinforced concrete walls several feet thick.**
   Engineered to resist explosions, fire, and other disasters, the fortification protects the treasure within.

8. **No public tours are allowed at Fort Knox.**
   Security concerns and confidentiality prevent civilian access, adding to the site's mystique.

9. **Fort Knox's gold is audited but has never been publicly counted in full detail.**
   Periodic audits confirm quantities but detailed records are closely held.

10. **The vault also houses a variety of valuable items beyond gold.**
    This includes important government documents, sensitive materials, and other precious assets.

11. **The complex includes barracks, training facilities, and support buildings for its guards.**
This ensures that security operations remain self-sustained on the base.

12. **Gold stored in Fort Knox underpins confidence in the U.S. dollar.**
Though the gold standard was abandoned decades ago, the reserves symbolize economic stability.

13. **The vault door requires a special time lock mechanism for access.**
Only authorized personnel assemble to open the door safely, following strict protocols.

14. **Fort Knox has never been successfully breached or compromised.**
Its reputation as an impregnable vault remains unchallenged through its history.

15. **The site was classified during World War II for protection against espionage and sabotage.**
Its security has only tightened since, reflecting its importance to national finance.

16. **The facility is encased within a 109,000-acre military reservation.**
This vast perimeter adds layers of defense well beyond the vault itself.

17. **Gold imported during the 1930s was consolidated here for safekeeping.**

Efforts during the Great Depression turned Fort Knox into a centralized depository.

18. **The vault is designed to be sealed indefinitely under emergency conditions.**
Its resilience makes it a stronghold even in national crises.

19. **Armored vehicles and security checkpoints surround Fort Knox.**
Physical, electronic, and human surveillance work in unison to monitor the area constantly.

20. **Fort Knox represents more than gold—it symbolizes the strength and security of the U.S. economy.**
Its image is synonymous worldwide with safety, trust, and financial power.

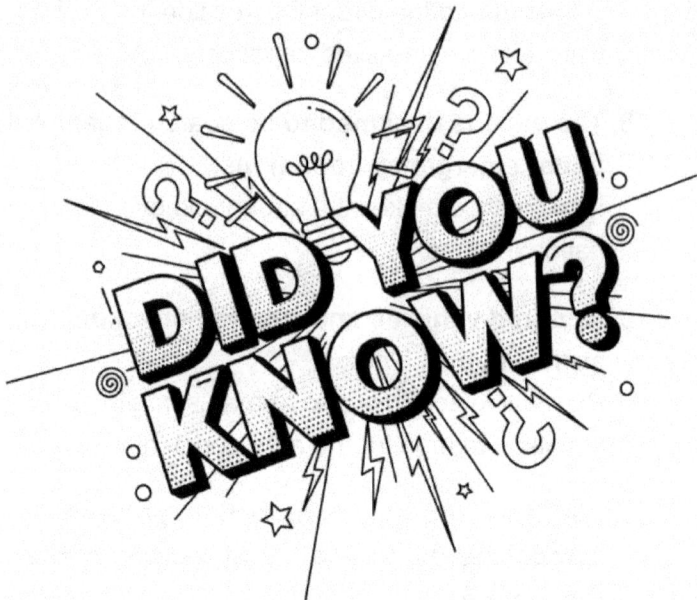

DID YOU KNOW?

- The vault door weighs more than four elephants combined.

- Gold bars in Fort Knox are stacked neatly in rows on metal pallets.

- Guards undergo rigorous security training and psychological evaluation.

- The facility also includes a chapel for personnel stationed there.

- Some gold stored dates back to the Gold Rush era.

- Fort Knox's security systems include motion detectors and seismic sensors.

- The entire vault complex is encased within layers of reinforced concrete.

- The vault's design allows for multi-day closure without external support.

8. Snake Island — Nature's No-Entry Zone

Off the Brazilian coast, Snake Island is a fortress of scales and fangs, home to the most venomous snakes on Earth. Forbidden, untamed, and lethal, it guards its secrets with a terrifying bite. Step carefully into the realm of this natural fortress, where survival and mystery intertwine in a deadly dance with nature.

FACTS

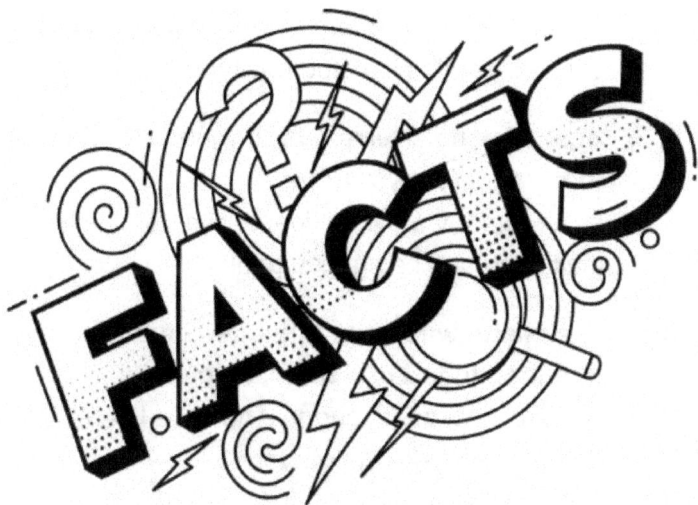

1. **Snake Island is home to the golden lancehead, one of the deadliest snakes on Earth.**
   This unique pit viper species evolved in isolation, with venom capable of causing rapid tissue damage and death.

2. **The island is off-limits to the public, protected by the Brazilian government.**
   Access is restricted to preserve the fragile ecosystem and prevent deadly encounters.

3. **Despite its small size, the island hosts thousands of venomous snakes.**
   Scientists estimate snake densities of up to five snakes per square meter in some areas.

4. **Golden lanceheads prey mainly on migratory birds that rest on the island.**

Adaptations allow them to hunt quickly and efficiently in this isolated environment.

5. **Snake Island's terrain is rugged, with dense forest and rocky outcrops.**
   Its geography provides ideal cover for snakes and makes human navigation perilous.

6. **The island was once inhabited centuries ago but abandoned due to snake density.**
   Historical accounts suggest humans left after dangerous snake encounters.

7. **Local fishermen regard the island as cursed and avoid approaching its shores.**
   Folklore mingles with reality to create a reputation of danger and superstition.

8. **The golden lancehead's venom is studied for medical potential, including blood pressure therapies.**
   Scientists analyze its unique proteins for promising pharmaceutical applications.

9. **Snake Island's snakes give birth to live young, an adaptation unlike many other reptiles.**
   This reproductive strategy suits the island's isolated environment.

10. **The island hosts rare plant species uniquely adapted to coexist with the snake population.**
    Its biodiversity is fragile but uniquely balanced.

11. **Visitors are only permitted for scientific research under strict safety protocols.**
Brazilian authorities enforce tight regulation to minimize human impact.

12. **The island is a critical site for herpetologists studying venom evolution.**
Its isolated population offers a living laboratory for evolutionary biology.

13. **The snakes' yellow-gold coloration camouflages them in the dry leaves and sand.**
This natural camouflage aids their ambush hunting technique.

14. **Snake Island was declared a protected area in the early 20th century.**
Conservation efforts focus on preserving the snake species from habitat degradation.

15. **No permanent human settlements exist due to the risk of venomous encounters.**
The island's natural hazards deter habitation.

16. **The island's perimeter is regularly patrolled by the Brazilian Navy.**
This prevents unauthorized visits and ensures safety measures are upheld.

17. **Snake Island has inspired documentaries, books, and popular culture references.**
Its deadly uniqueness fascinates wildlife enthusiasts globally.

18. **The golden lancehead's venom is up to five times more potent than mainland relatives.**
Its evolutionary path led to increased toxicity due to its specialized diet.

19. **The island also provides critical breeding grounds for various seabird species.**
Seabirds withstand snake predation in niche safe zones.

20. **Snake Island exemplifies nature's raw evolutionary forces and isolation effects.**
It stands as one of the most fascinating and lethal ecosystems on the planet.

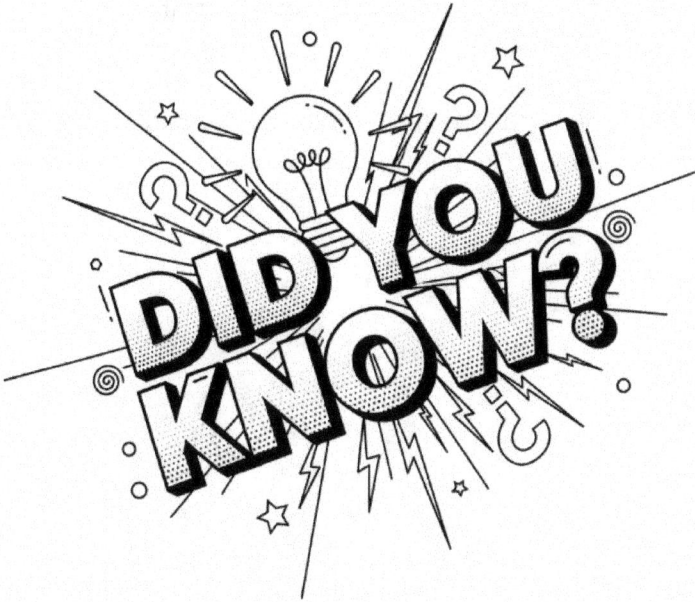

- Snake densities on the island can reach one snake per square meter.

- Their venom contains unique proteins not found in other snakes.

- No known recorded human deaths on the island, but severe bites are highly dangerous.

- The island is often called "Island of Death" due to its lethal residents.

- The snakes evolved from mainland species isolated for thousands of years.

- The island is 33 km off the coast of Brazil in the Atlantic Ocean.

- The golden lancehead feeds primarily on migratory birds and small rodents.

- The Brazilian government restricts access to protect both humans and snakes.

9. North Korea's Restricted Borders

The borders of North Korea are less borders and more impervious walls, shrouded in secrecy and strict control. These lines cut through mountains and rivers, blocking escape and isolating a nation steeped in mystery. Peel back the layers of surveillance, defense, and human struggle beyond these guarded edges.

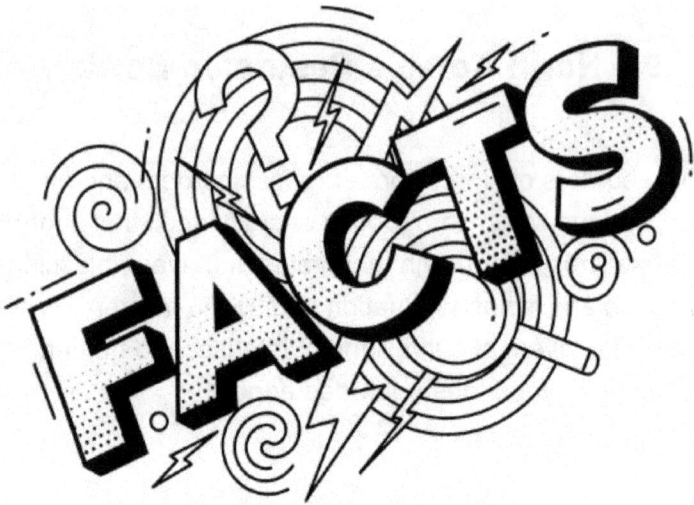

1. **North Korea tightly controls its borders, heavily restricting all movement.**
   The regime enforces strict border security to prevent unauthorized entry and escape, making it one of the most closed borders in the world.

2. **The demilitarized zone (DMZ) between North and South Korea is a heavily fortified buffer zone.**
   At approximately 250 kilometers long and 4 kilometers wide, it is lined with landmines, barbed wire, and armed guards.

3. **Escape from North Korea is perilous, with severe consequences for defectors.**
   Those caught attempting to flee face harsh punishments, including imprisonment, torture, or execution.

4. **Thousands of soldiers and police officers patrol the borders daily.**
   Constant vigilance ensures surveillance and control over unauthorized crossings.

5. **The Chinese border also features tight controls, with networks of fences and patrols.**
   Despite this, thousands of defectors use China as a transit point to seek asylum abroad.

6. **North Korea issues strict travel restrictions even internally.**
   Citizens require permission and travel documents to move between provinces or cities.

7. **The border security is supported by advanced technologies, including CCTV and drones.**
   These systems help authorities monitor movement and prevent escapes.

8. **The regime uses harsh propaganda and severe penalties to discourage border violations.**
   Fear is a key instrument in maintaining border control and loyalty.

9. **Defectors risk crossing rivers, mountains, and dangerous terrain to flee.**
   Natural obstacles compound the physical risks of illegal border crossings.

10. **Attempted defections by military personnel are among the most dangerous.**

Soldiers caught defecting face capital punishment for treason.

11. **The border with South Korea is one of the most heavily militarized on Earth.**
The DMZ remains a tense flashpoint between the two countries, monitored by both sides.

12. **Border villages on the North Korean side often face restrictions and surveillance.**
Residents are watched closely to prevent collusion or escape attempts.

13. **Trade and communication across the borders are heavily restricted and monitored.**
Official crossings are limited to tightly controlled checkpoints.

14. **The border's rugged and forested terrain aids and complicates surveillance efforts.**
While offering cover for defectors, the environment also limits patrol mobility.

15. **Several high-profile escapes have occurred, gaining international attention.**
These stories often highlight the desperation and bravery of defectors.

16. **The regime funds expanded border control infrastructure periodically.**
Upgrades in fencing, surveillance, and troops reflect an ongoing emphasis on security.

17. **The borders also serve as psychological barriers, reinforced by ideological**

indoctrination.
Citizens are taught to fear and distrust outside influences beyond the borders.

18. **Cross-border smuggling continues despite strict regulations.**
Illegal goods, information, and small numbers of people move secretly across frontiers.

19. **International efforts to assist defectors include covert aid networks inside China.**
Human rights groups work to rescue and resettle those fleeing the regime.

20. **North Korea's borders remain vital instruments for regime preservation.**
Strong control ensures regime survival by limiting external influences and population flow.

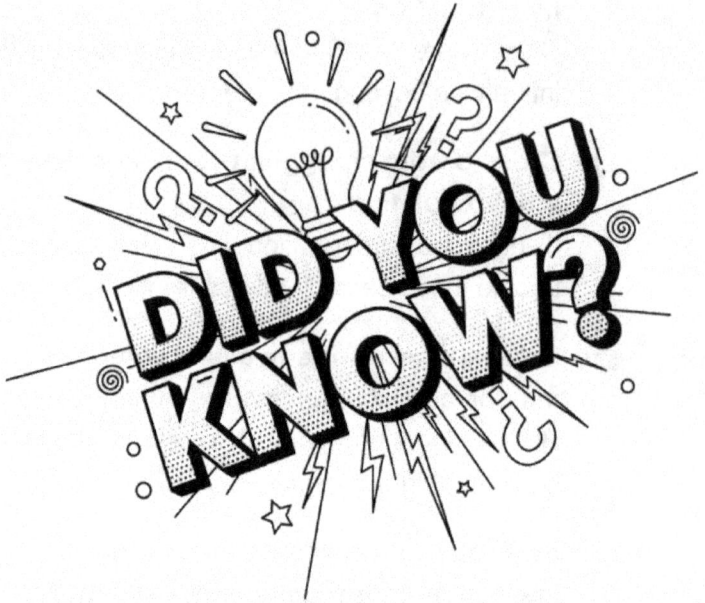
DID YOU KNOW?

- The DMZ is often called the "most dangerous border in the world."

- There is an unresolved border dispute that fuels occasional skirmishes.

- North Korea restricts citizens from owning passports or traveling abroad.

- The regime runs informant networks within border regions.

- Many defectors cross frozen rivers during winter.

- The Chinese border includes high-tech sensors and cameras.

- Propaganda pamphlets are sometimes floated across borders.

- Several countries operate refugee operations focused on North Korean defectors.

10. Mezhgorye — The Hidden Russian Town

Tucked away in the remote Urals, Mezhgorye is a phantom city, whispered about but rarely seen. Cloaked in the shadows of Cold War secrets and nuclear mystery, it guards Kremlin's darkest projects. Unlock the enigma of this remote fortress and the secrets its walls conceal.

1. **Mezhgorye is a secretive closed town in Russia believed to serve military or nuclear functions.**
   Its existence was officially unacknowledged for years and it remains off-limits to foreigners.

2. **The town is located in Bashkortostan near the Ural Mountains.**
   It is isolated geographically and administratively classified as a closed city.

3. **Mezhgorye reportedly hosts nuclear weapon storage or development facilities.**
   Analysts speculate it supports Russia's strategic missile and nuclear programs.

4. **The town has tightly controlled access, with fencing and checkpoints.**
   Travel in and out is monitored; outsiders require special permits.

5. **Mezhgorye features modern residential and community facilities for residents.**
   Despite secrecy, the town functions as a self-contained urban area.

6. **Its population is estimated between 15,000 and 20,000 people, mostly workers and their families.**
   Residents often have ties to defense or intelligence agencies.

7. **Satellite images reveal stark security infrastructure including barriers and guard posts.**
   These features reinforce access restrictions and secrecy.

8. **The town was built during the Soviet era, likely as a response to Cold War military needs.**
   Its design and location reflect strategic security considerations.

9. **Residents are subject to strict rules on communication and foreign contact.**
   Confidentiality is mandatory to protect sensitive operations.

10. **Maps often omit Mezhgorye, labeling it as either "closed" or unmarked.**
    This standard practice hides controversial or secret installations.

11. **The town reportedly includes manufacturing plants related to strategic weaponry.**
Local industries are believed to produce components for nuclear delivery systems.

12. **Public information about Mezhgorye is limited by government censorship.**
Russian news media rarely cover the town, enhancing its mystique.

13. **There are rumors the town has underground bunkers and storage facilities.**
These structures likely house sensitive materials requiring extreme protection.

14. **Mezhgorye has its own utilities and infrastructure to remain self-sufficient.**
This ensures continuity of operations even during emergencies.

15. **The town's official postal code and physical address are classified.**
This prevents correspondence that could reveal information about its operations.

16. **Satellite monitoring by foreign intelligence tracks Mezhgorye's developments regularly.**
This surveillance informs geopolitical assessments globally.

17. **Some defectors and insiders have reportedly leaked limited information about life within.**
Accounts emphasize the town's strict security and closed society.

18. **Mezhgorye symbolizes Russia's continued investment in strategic military assets.**
The town's secrecy reflects the enduring importance of nuclear deterrence.

19. **Its remote mountain location also aids confidentiality and reduces risk of espionage.**
Natural geography enhances its security profile.

20. **Despite secrecy, Mezhgorye's presence is a crucial element in global nuclear nonproliferation talks.**
Understanding its role helps international agencies monitor arms control compliance.

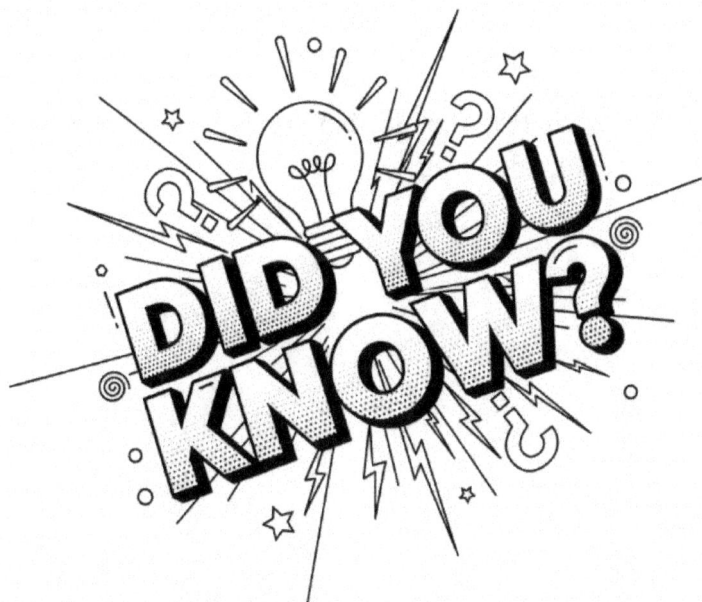

- Mezhgorye was not shown on Russian maps until the 1990s.

- The town operates its own schools, hospitals, and shops for residents.

- No telephone directories or public records are available for Mezhgorye.

- The surrounding region is rich in mineral resources linked to strategic industries.

- Residents are often recruited directly from military academies.

- The town's infrastructure includes extensive underground tunnels.

- Mezhgorye's name is derived from 'between mountains' in Russian.

- Satellite images indicate expansion and modernization of facilities continue.

11. Room 39 — North Korea's Secret Economy

Behind the iron curtain of North Korea's regime exists Room 39—a shadowy web spinning illicit wealth in service of secrets and power. It hides in the shadows of global finance, funding ambitions that defy sanctions and scrutiny. Enter the covert world where money flows unseen, and the stakes are survival and supremacy.

1. **Room 39 is a shadowy North Korean entity responsible for generating foreign currency through illicit means.**
   Allegedly founded in the 1970s, it orchestrates black market activities to fund the regime's leadership and military.

2. **The organization oversees activities like counterfeiting, drug smuggling, and arms sales.**
   Room 39 manages covert enterprises crucial for circumventing international sanctions.

3. **Estimates suggest its illicit revenue could reach billions annually.**
   These funds support North Korea's nuclear weapons program and elite privileges.

4. **The group operates through a network of front companies and overseas agents.**

These entities mask its involvement in global financial systems.

5. **Luxury goods procurement and currency trading are part of its portfolio.**
   Room 39 supplies the elite with Western luxuries to maintain regime loyalty.

6. **International agencies attempt to disrupt Room 39 operations but face challenges.**
   Its secrecy, sophisticated laundering, and state protection complicate enforcement.

7. **Room 39 is believed to have facilitated cybercrime operations, including ransomware attacks.**
   These digital operations supplement traditional illicit trades.

8. **The organization is tightly controlled at the highest government level.**
   Directives come reportedly from the inner circle of the ruling regime.

9. **Smuggling routes span land, sea, and air, often via China and Southeast Asia.**
   These paths supply avenues for contraband and illegal goods worldwide.

10. **The group avoids diplomatic and commercial channels, operating underground.**
    Its invisibility makes tracing and disrupting finances difficult.

11. **Room 39 also funds domestic projects considered critical by the regime.**
Infrastructure developments and military upgrades benefit from its revenue streams.

12. **Bank accounts linked to Room 39 have been frozen or sanctioned by various countries.**
Efforts to isolate it financially have met with limited, partial success.

13. **The group involves foreign nationals working in cooperation with North Korean officials.**
These collaborations help bypass financial restrictions internationally.

14. **Human rights organizations highlight Room 39 as a node funding oppressive activities.**
Money raised contributes directly or indirectly to the perpetuation of human rights abuses.

15. **Room 39's complexity has increased with digital finance and cryptocurrency use.**
New technologies enable more covert transactions and international reach.

16. **The opaque nature of North Korea's financial controls aids Room 39's secrecy.**
Limited transparency prevents global oversight of the regime's budget and income.

17. **The organization has links to other known illicit entities across Asia.**
Cross-border criminal networks cooperate in money laundering and trafficking.

18. **Despite sanctions, the regime's foreign currency coffers remain robust.**
Room 39's activities help sustain economic resilience against international pressure.

19. **Whistleblowers and defectors provide valuable intelligence about Room 39 operations.**
Their testimonies reveal the organization's methods and scale.

20. **Room 39 embodies the nexus of North Korea's economic survival strategy amid isolation.**
Its covert revenue streams buttress the regime's endurance in a globalized world.

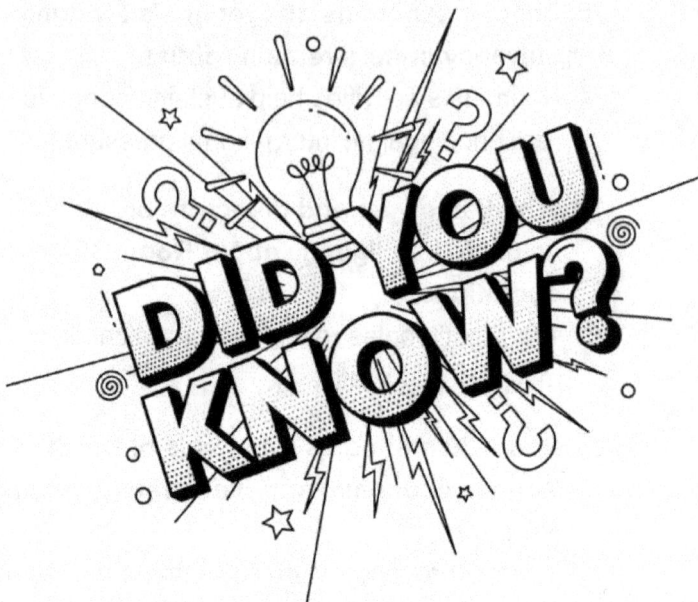

- Room 39 allegedly owns multiple luxury hotels in Pyongyang.

- It reportedly operated a counterfeit $100 bill factory in China.

- The organization is known also as "Bureau 39."

- Cyber thefts linked to Room 39 have netted millions in illicit funds.

- It controls several foreign trade companies fronting illicit operations.

- Room 39 aids funding for North Korea's nuclear weapons program.

- It utilizes cryptocurrency exchanges to launder money.

- Many countries have imposed sanctions targeting Room 39's affiliates.

12. Pine Gap — Australia's Eavesdropping Base

In a remote Australian desert, Pine Gap listens to the whispers of the world. This joint U.S.-Australian base controls satellites that spy on signals far beyond the horizon, mapping secrets in silence. Explore the high-tech heart of global surveillance, where privacy fades and power listens.

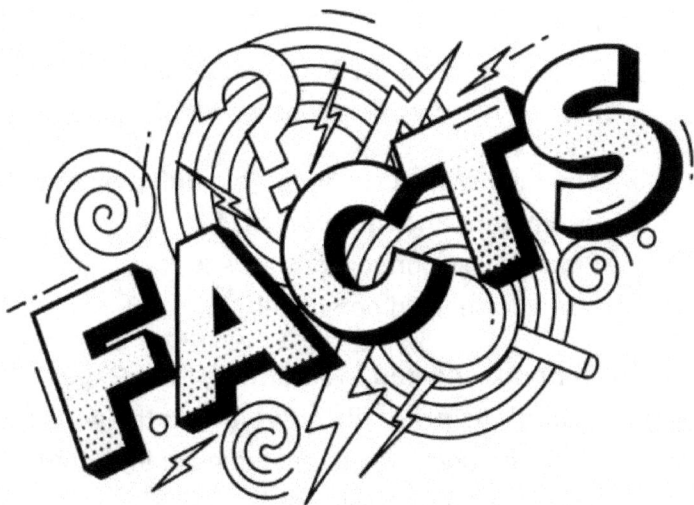

1. **Pine Gap is a joint U.S.-Australian satellite surveillance and intelligence-gathering station near Alice Springs.**
   Established in 1970, it plays a critical role in signals intelligence and global communications monitoring.

2. **The base controls several key satellites used for spying and missile warning.**
   Its remote desert location provides ideal conditions for satellite tracking and control.

3. **Pine Gap operates as a central hub for electronic eavesdropping on foreign communications.**
   It intercepts signals from Asia, the Middle East, and beyond, aiding intelligence agencies.

4. **Technologies operated at Pine Gap include radar systems and telecommunications**

intercepts.
These provide warnings of missile launches and support military operations worldwide.

5. **The facility is surrounded by multiple security perimeters and monitored 24/7.**
Strict access controls protect sensitive technologies and personnel.

6. **Although located in Australia, Pine Gap's operations primarily serve U.S. intelligence.**
This partnership is a cornerstone of the 'Five Eyes' intelligence alliance.

7. **Satellite telecommunications data passed through Pine Gap fuel international espionage.**
Operations reportedly involve hacking, cyber war support, and global monitoring.

8. **Pine Gap's presence remains somewhat controversial among Australians due to perceived sovereignty concerns.**
Debates continue over the balance of alliance benefits versus strategic risks.

9. **The base contributes intelligence sharing to key U.S. defense initiatives.**
It enhances global situational awareness and counter-terrorism operations.

10. **Pine Gap supports real-time battlefield communications and satellite navigation systems.**

This integration aids allied military deployments worldwide.

11. **Its personnel include both Australian Defence Force members and U.S. intelligence operatives.**
The combined staff rely on shared protocols and strict security measures.

12. **The base has undergone upgrades over the decades to incorporate advanced technology.**
This maintains it as one of the pinnacle satellite and signals intelligence facilities globally.

13. **Pine Gap is equipped with spherical radomes housing satellite dishes.**
These protect invaluable antenna arrays from the harsh desert environment while allowing uninterrupted operations.

14. **The site's strategic location allows interception of over a third of the world's satellite communications.**
Its intelligence reach is global and highly sensitive.

15. **Environmental and cultural concerns have been raised regarding the base's impacts.**
Indigenous groups and environmentalists occasionally petition for changes and transparency.

16. **Pine Gap is linked to controversial surveillance programs revealed in global**

leaks.
These disclosures amplified public debates over privacy and intelligence collection.

17. **The Australian government carefully regulates information about Pine Gap.**
Official statements acknowledge cooperation but limit operational disclosures.

18. **Satellite communications management at Pine Gap supports both defense and intelligence missions.**
This dual role increases its strategic importance.

19. **Analysts consider Pine Gap critical to intelligence on regional rivals, including China and Russia.**
Its capabilities provide early warning and diplomatic leverage.

20. **Pine Gap's ongoing upgrades include integration with space-based missile defense systems.**
This aligns with expanding U.S. and allied focus on space warfare capabilities.

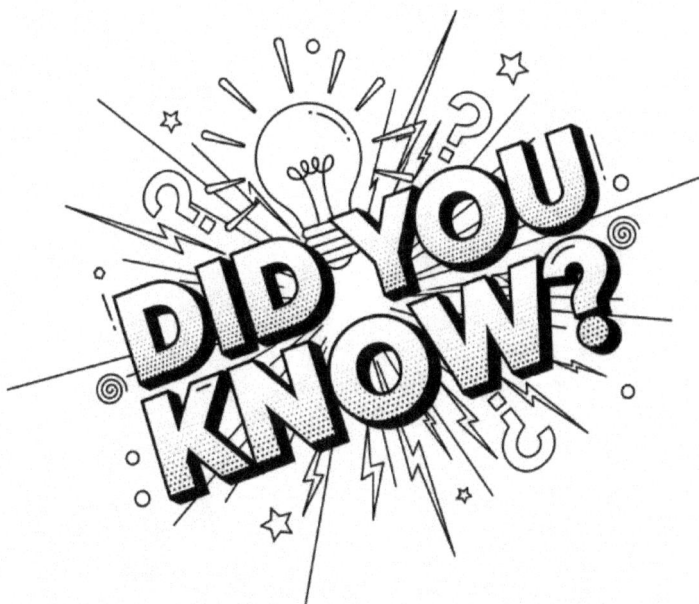

DID YOU KNOW?

- Pine Gap is sometimes called "The Ranch" by operatives.

- The base employs more than 800 personnel.

- It controls satellites used for missile launch detection.

- The facility operates around the clock, 365 days a year.

- Pine Gap's journey began during Cold War tensions.

- Indigenous groups near Alice Springs have expressed concerns over the facility.

- Pine Gap also monitors undersea cables via satellite links.

- The base was featured in the TV series "Pine Gap," exploring intelligence drama.

13. The Island of Hashima — Japan's Ghost Stronghold

Concrete towers loom on a tiny island off the coast of Japan, relics of a booming coal mining era now frozen in silence. Hashima's abandoned dwellings whisper stories of industrial might and forgotten lives. Traverse this ghostly cityscape and uncover the ruins of humanity's relentless march forward.

1. **Hashima Island, also known as Battleship Island, was a bustling coal mining facility until 1974.**
   Once housing thousands, it became a symbol of rapid industrialization and later abandonment.

2. **The island's nickname comes from its shape resembling a battleship.**
   Its densely packed concrete buildings crowded a tiny island just 480 meters long.

3. **At its peak, Hashima had one of the highest population densities worldwide.**
   Around 5,000 residents lived in its compact, fortress-like community—miners and their families.

4. **The coal mining industry fueled Japan's modernization during the 20th century.**

Hashima contributed significantly to energy supplies crucial for industrial growth.

5. **Harsh working conditions and overcrowding marked life on the island.**
   Workers labored underground while living in cramped apartments with minimal facilities.

6. **In 1974, the mines closed due to petroleum replacing coal in energy production.**
   The island was abandoned almost overnight, leaving behind ruins frozen in time.

7. **Hashima remained off-limits for decades due to safety risks from crumbling infrastructure.**
   Many buildings fell into disrepair, making the island a dangerous ghost town.

8. **The island was opened partially to tourists in 2009 after stabilization efforts.**
   Visitors can now explore certain areas under guided supervision.

9. **Hashima is a UNESCO World Heritage Site recognizing its industrial heritage.**
   This designation highlights its historical significance and need for preservation.

10. **The island became emblematic of Japan's rapid industrial transformation.**
    It symbolizes both economic progress and the human cost of resource extraction.

11. **Films such as "Skyfall" have used Hashima as a dramatic location.**

Its haunting, abandoned structures offer a stark, cinematic backdrop.

12. **Many Hashima residents were forcibly conscripted laborers, including Koreans and Chinese during WWII.**
This dark part of history is the subject of ongoing debates about wartime responsibilities.

13. **The island features tall concrete apartment blocks designed to withstand typhoons.**
Its architecture reflects a blend of urban density and industrial necessity.

14. **Hashima's pier and seawall protect it from the rough waters of the East China Sea.**
These barriers also contributed to its battleship-like silhouette.

15. **The mining tunnels beneath the island stretch for kilometers underwater.**
Submerged infrastructure poses additional hazards but fascinates explorers and historians.

16. **Several preservation projects aim to keep Hashima safe for future generations.**
Efforts focus on stabilizing ruins while acknowledging its complex history.

17. **Hashima's school and hospital buildings served the community until abandonment.**
Artifacts inside remain, telling stories of island life long ceased.

18. **The island's closure led to an economic and social collapse for its inhabitants.**
Displaced residents moved to mainland cities, marking the end of an era.

19. **Hashima's population peaked in the 1950s during Japan's economic boom.**
It was a bright center of industrial labor during its heyday.

20. **Today, Hashima stands as a poignant reminder of industrialization's rise and fall.**
Its stark ruins attract tourists and historians interested in industrial heritage and memory.

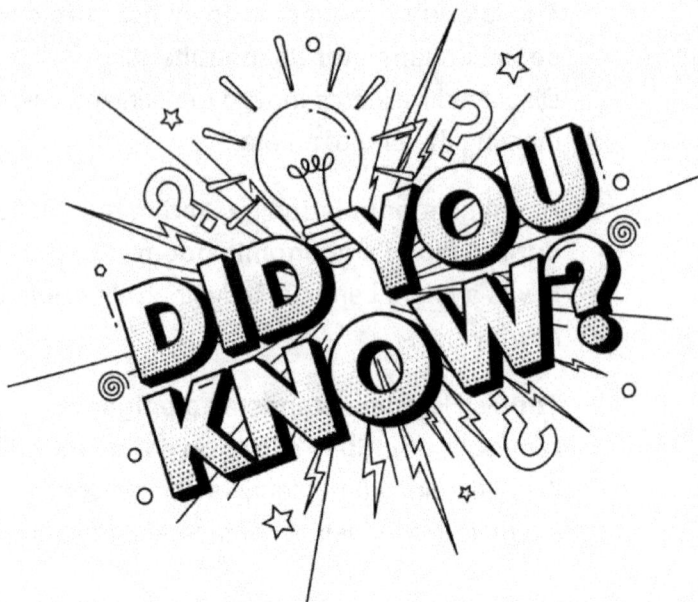
DID YOU KNOW?

- Hashima once had Japan's first concrete high-rise apartment buildings.

- The island's seawall was built to protect it from typhoon waves.

- Coal mining underground continued until 1974 despite surface decline.

- The island remained uninhabited for decades after closure.

- Hashima hosts memorials remembering forced wartime laborers.

- The island inspired a UNESCO listing for industrial heritage.

- Its abandoned buildings appear in multiple films and documentaries.

- Few remaining residents visit for reunions and commemorations.

14. Mount Weather — The American Doomsday Bunker

Beneath Virginia's rocky hills lies Mount Weather—a fortress designed to preserve America's government through catastrophe and chaos. Cloaked in secrecy and steel, it stands ready for the worst, a hidden sanctuary from disaster. Descend into the depths of this doomsday refuge and uncover its chilling purpose.

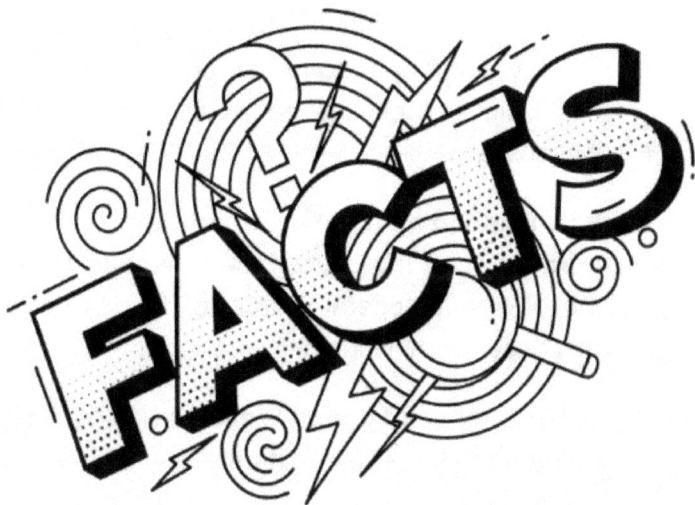

1. **Mount Weather is a classified government facility serving as a critical emergency operations center.**
   Located in Virginia, it acts as a secure refuge and command post during national crises.

2. **It was developed during the Cold War for continuity of government operations.**
   Its purpose is to safeguard U.S. leadership and essential functions amid catastrophic events.

3. **The facility is partially underground, encased in reinforced concrete and rock.**
   This design protects against nuclear blasts, biological threats, and natural disasters.

4. **Mount Weather has a secretive population of staff and government personnel.**
   Staff includes emergency planners, communications experts, and defense leaders.

5. **The site contains living quarters, medical facilities, and command centers.**
It is designed for sustained occupation in isolation if necessary.

6. **It is linked to national emergency infrastructure including FEMA management.**
Mount Weather operates as a hub for disaster response coordination and recovery.

7. **The existence of Mount Weather was publicly revealed in the 1970s but details remain classified.**
Its exact layout and capabilities are closely guarded secrets.

8. **The facility has helicopter pads and underground tunnels connecting to other secure sites.**
These provide critical transportation and communication channels during emergencies.

9. **Mount Weather plays a role in chemical, biological, radiological, and nuclear defense.**
It is equipped to monitor and respond to various homeland security threats.

10. **The facility supports communication with other bunkers like Raven Rock and Cheyenne Mountain.**
This network ensures command continuity over military and civilian operations.

11. **Mount Weather has been used in numerous national emergency drills and exercises.**
These tests validate readiness for crises ranging from terrorist attacks to natural disasters.

12. **Its secure underground areas include data centers housing classified information.**
Protection of sensitive government data is a key function.

13. **The site extends above and below Mount Weather's surface, covering significant acreage.**
This bagdelimits residential and operational zones for its population and functions.

14. **Access is restricted to authorized personnel with top-level clearances.**
The isolated nature underscores its function as a government last-resort shelter.

15. **The facility is equipped with backup utilities for power, water, and air filtration.**
This ensures survivability in the event of infrastructure collapse outside.

16. **Mount Weather remains an active asset in the U.S.'s national security and emergency strategy.**
Its readiness supports survival and governance continuity under extreme conditions.

17. **The site reportedly includes advanced communications equipment for satellite and**

ground-based links.
Robust communication is essential for coordinated crisis response.

18. **Historical use has extended to hosting displaced officials during natural disasters and threats.**
It has functioned experimentally in real-world contingencies.

19. **Mount Weather's secrecy has inspired fiction and conspiracy theories about government bunkers.**
Nonetheless, it remains critical for maintaining government stability.

20. **Modern upgrades ensure it can meet 21st-century threats, including cyber-attacks.**
Continuous improvements maintain its strategic importance.

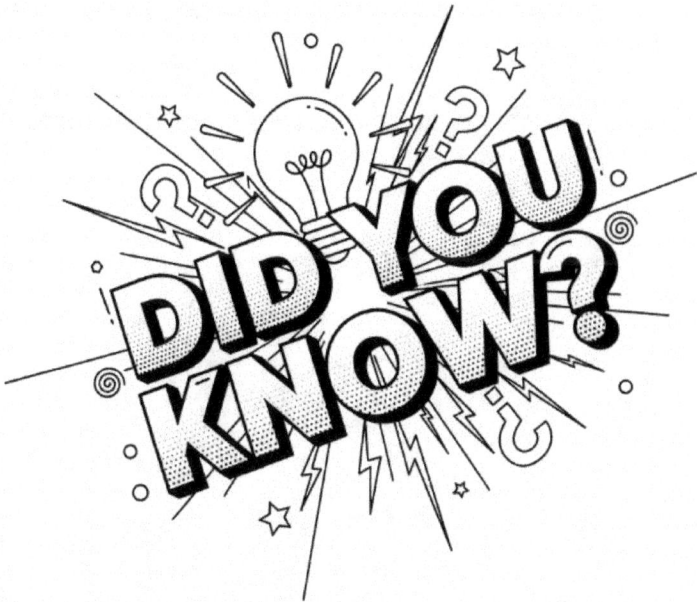

DID YOU KNOW?

- The facility's name is often used to refer broadly to government continuity bunkers.

- It houses an emergency operations center that can activate within minutes.

- Employees must regularly undergo emergency preparedness training.

- Its location was chosen due to natural protection by the Blue Ridge Mountains.

- Mount Weather has contingency plans for evacuating the White House.

- The complex is divided into "mounts" indicating different sectors of the site.

- It maintains a power plant capable of independent operation.

- A network of tunnels connects it to other secret government locations.

15. Niihau — Hawaii's Private Island

Known as the "Forbidden Island," Niihau remains one of
the few places untouched by modern life. Owned
privately and fiercely protected, it's a sanctuary of native
Hawaiian culture and pristine wilderness. Step back in
time to a place where ancient traditions survive beneath
tropical skies.

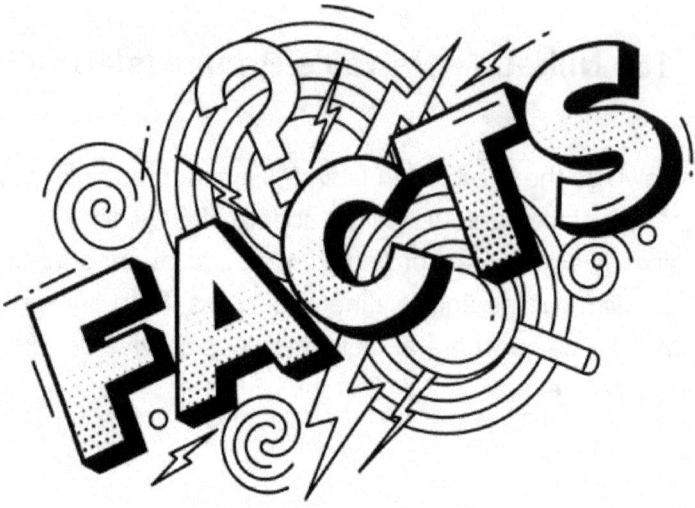
FACTS

1. **Niihau is a privately owned island in Hawaii known for its isolation and limited access.**
   Owned by the Robinson family since 1864, visitors must have permission to visit and few outsiders ever do.

2. **It is nicknamed the "Forbidden Island" because of restricted tourism and development.**
   This policy preserves the island's traditional Hawaiian culture and environment.

3. **Niihau has a population of around 170 native Hawaiians living primarily a subsistence lifestyle.**
   Residents maintain traditional practices including fishing, hunting, and weaving.

4. **The island has no paved roads and limited modern infrastructure.**

This contributes to its remote, undeveloped character.

5. **Residents speak Hawaiian as their first language, making Niihau one of the few Hawaiian-speaking communities.**
   The island is pivotal in preserving native language and customs.

6. **Niihau is home to unique fauna, including the endangered Hawaiian monk seal.**
   Conservation efforts protect the island's natural ecosystems.

7. **Visitors require invitation or special permits to access the island.**
   Tourism is heavily restricted to minimize cultural and environmental impact.

8. **Air and boat travel are the only ways to reach Niihau, emphasizing isolation.**
   Commercial transport is almost nonexistent, maintaining privacy and seclusion.

9. **The island played a role in WWII, serving as a lookout post against potential enemy attacks.**
   Its strategic location made it important for military surveillance.

10. **Niihau's residents maintain traditional festivals and ceremonies reflecting ancient Hawaiian heritage.**
    These cultural activities are central to community identity and continuity.

11. **The Robinson family governs social and land use policies strictly.**
This preserves Niihau's character but limits economic development.

12. **The island's land is mostly volcanic terrain with beautiful beaches and coral reefs.**
Its geography supports diverse marine life and habitat.

13. **Large parts of Niihau are designated as wildlife sanctuaries.**
These preserve nesting grounds for birds and turtles.

14. **Fishing and hunting are primary food sources for residents.**
Traditional techniques sustain subsistence economies.

15. **Electricity and modern technology are minimal outside of a few community buildings.**
This supports a low-impact lifestyle aligning with natural rhythms.

16. **Niihau's community governance blends native customs with modern necessities.**
Leaders manage the island's resources while respecting ancestral traditions.

17. **Rare plants endemic to Niihau contribute to its ecological significance.**

Scientists study these species for conservation and biodiversity.

18. **The island's beaches attract a small number of permitted visitors for snorkeling and nature study.**
Strict environmental guidelines govern these visits.

19. **Niihau's isolation has helped shield it from many invasive species affecting other Hawaiian Islands.**
This results in a comparatively pristine natural environment.

20. **The island represents a unique blend of private ownership, cultural preservation, and environmental stewardship.**
Niihau offers a rare, living example of maintaining indigenous ways in the modern age.

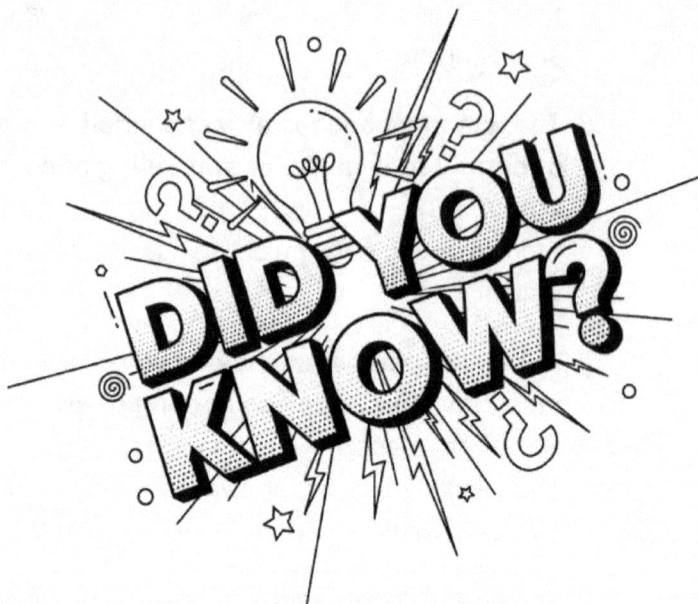
DID YOU KNOW?

- Niihau is 70 square kilometers, one of the smaller Hawaiian Islands.

- Hawaiian radio broadcasts are popular and promote local traditions.

- The island's main settlement is called Puʻuwai, the westernmost community in the U.S.

- Niihau shells were once used for traditional jewelry and trade.

- The island has no public roads, only dirt paths and trails.

- Traditional Hawaiian crafts are still made exclusively by locals.

- Niihau's coral reefs provide habitat for over 200 fish species.

- The island hosts rituals honoring ancient Hawaiian gods and spirits.

16. The Doomsday Seed Vault — Svalbard, Norway

In the icy vaults of Svalbard, millions of seeds lie dormant, silently guarding the future of humanity's food supply. Shielded by permafrost and isolation, this seed vault is a vault of hope against global calamity. Enter this Arctic fortress where life's legacy is frozen, waiting for tomorrow.

1. **The Svalbard Global Seed Vault is a secure underground facility storing millions of seed samples.**
   Located on a remote Arctic island, it acts as the world's backup repository for the world's crop diversity.

2. **Opened in 2008, the vault protects seeds from global catastrophes affecting agriculture.**
   It safeguards humanity's food security in the face of climate change, war, and natural disasters.

3. **The vault stores seeds from nearly every country, representing thousands of plant species.**
   This resource preserves essential genetic diversity for future plant breeding and research.

4. **Seeds are deposited by international gene banks and governments.**

The vault serves as a failsafe storage for collections stored elsewhere.

5. **Svalbard's permafrost and cold climate provide ideal conditions for seed preservation.**
   Natural freezing maintains seed viability without reliance on mechanical cooling.

6. **The vault is built inside a mountain to maximize security and protection.**
   It can withstand nuclear war, natural disasters, and technological failures.

7. **Entrance requires high-level approval and strict protocols.**
   Only authorized curators manage seed deposits and withdrawals.

8. **The vault serves as insurance for global food supply resilience.**
   Its genetic materials can aid in restoring crops after epidemics or climate disruptions.

9. **Svalbard is politically stable, minimizing risks of conflict affecting the vault.**
   Norway's governance ensures long-term protection and neutrality.

10. **The vault has over a million seed samples representing important staple crops.**
    This includes wheat, rice, corn, and ancient grains essential for global diets.

11. **It is funded by the Norwegian government and supported by international organizations.**
Collaborative management underscores its global importance.

12. **The vault is designed to function even without power for extended periods.**
Permafrost and insulation naturally preserve the frozen seed beds.

13. **Seeds deposited must be healthy, genetically pure, and verifiably viable.**
Strict quality controls maintain the integrity of genetic material.

14. **International treaties encourage countries to contribute and utilize the vault.**
It acts as a shared resource for global agricultural resilience.

15. **In 2015, seeds were withdrawn for the first time to restore collections damaged in conflict.**
This demonstrated the vault's vital real-world role.

16. **The vault is monitored remotely and physically inspected regularly.**
Security and environmental integrity are top priorities.

17. **Some seeds stored date back centuries or represent endangered crop varieties.**
Conservation of rare diversity is critical for future food sources.

18. **Climate change threatens permafrost, prompting vault construction with extra protective features.**
Engineers designed it for long-term adaptation.

19. **The vault is a symbol of global cooperation in food security and biodiversity conservation.**
It exemplifies humanity's commitment to preserving nature's genetic heritage.

20. **Svalbard's remote location requires careful logistics for seed transport and storage.**
Seeds travel via specialty carriers under controlled conditions to reach the vault.

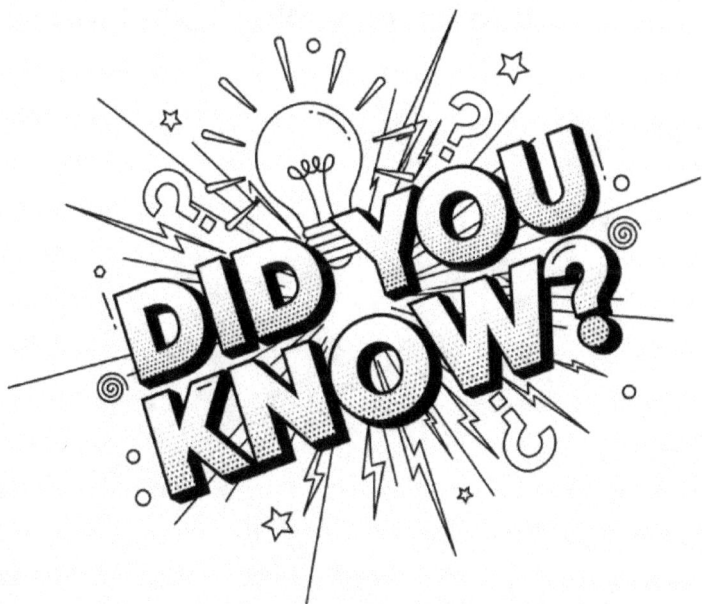
DID YOU KNOW?

- The vault is nicknamed the "Doomsday Vault."

- It stores seeds from over 5,000 plant species worldwide.

- Entrance doors are secured behind multiple heavy steel blast doors.

- Seeds are stored in specially sealed, vacuum-packed containers.

- The facility's entry tunnel is designed to protect against radiological contamination.

- Backup generators ensure cooling even during power failures.

- Svalbard's extreme weather further deters unauthorized access.

- The vault is built to last for at least a millennium.

17. Woomera Prohibited Area — Australia's Hidden Range

Spanning thousands of square kilometers, Woomera is a vast, secretive testing ground for weapons and aerospace technology. Hidden in the outback, it's a proving ground where innovation meets military might. Explore the desert range that shapes tomorrow's defense in silence and sand.

1. **The Woomera Prohibited Area (WPA) is one of the largest land-based military testing ranges globally.**
   Located in South Australia, it spans over 122,000 square kilometers and is used for weapons and aerospace testing.

2. **Established in 1947, the WPA originally supported British missile and rocket development.**
   The range contributed to pioneering research during the nascent years of aerospace technology.

3. **The WPA is actively used by the Australian Defence Force for weapons testing.**
   Tests include missile firings, electronic warfare trials, and aircraft systems evaluation.

4. **Access to the WPA is strictly controlled with checkpoints and patrols.**
   Restriction zones ensure civilians are kept clear during live testing operations.

5. **The area includes multiple permanent military facilities including airstrips and control centers.**
   These support sustained research and rapid response capabilities.

6. **Woomera's vast desert environment provides ample space for high-velocity missile launches.**
   Its isolation and size make it ideal for tracking long-range weapons.

7. **International defense collaborators, including the U.S. and UK, have utilized the WPA.**
   Multinational cooperation has enhanced testing capacity and interoperability.

8. **The range includes advanced tracking radars and telemetry stations.**
   These systems monitor and analyze test flights with high precision.

9. **WPA encompasses culturally significant Aboriginal lands, leading to ongoing land use negotiations.**
   Efforts to balance defense priorities and indigenous rights continue.

10. **The range supports both manned and unmanned aerial vehicle testing.**
Drones and pilotless aircraft are increasingly vital to contemporary military exercises.

11. **The WPA has been pivotal in developing anti-ballistic missile technology.**
Research here contributes to global missile defense strategies.

12. **Environmental monitoring programs operate within the range.**
These track ecological impacts and promote sustainability where possible.

13. **The vast WPA often disrupts nearby civilian airspace during active tests.**
Coordination with aviation authorities minimizes interference.

14. **Live-fire exercises often require temporary exclusion zones extending over hundreds of kilometers.**
This ensures public safety during hazardous operations.

15. **Woomera's history includes rocket launches and satellite testing in Australia's early space program.**
This legacy marks the site as a pioneer in aerospace technology.

16. **Security includes restricted road access and surveillance, preventing unauthorized entry.**

The remoteness and strict measures protect sensitive testing.

17. **Personnel at the range include scientists, military technicians, and range safety officers.** Their expertise enables complex, high-risk operations in safety protocols.

18. **The WPA contributes to Australia's national security and technological independence.** It supports research protecting strategic military assets.

19. **The range's desert terrain is used for training ground troops alongside technology testing.** This dual function enhances operational readiness.

20. **Woomera remains one of the world's premier testing facilities for aerospace and defense industries.** Its role continues to evolve with emerging defense technologies and geopolitical demands.

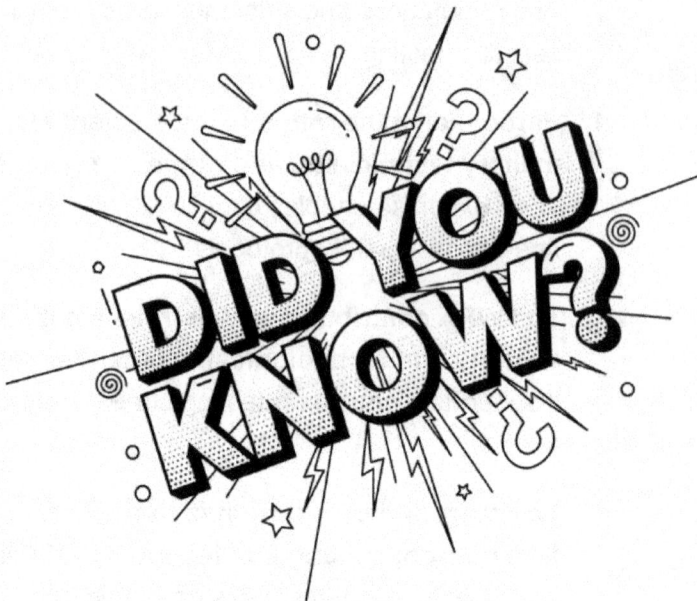

- Woomera's test flights reach altitudes of hundreds of kilometers.

- Over 4,000 military personnel have been involved in WPA operations historically.

- The site has been used for early satellite launch missions.

- Indigenous communities have cultural heritage sites within WPA boundaries.

- The range is named after an Aboriginal spear-thrower tool.

- WPA tests help develop missile interception and tracking systems.

- The area includes vast unpopulated desert ideal for classified operations.

- WPA collaborates extensively with allied foreign defense agencies.

18. The Chernobyl Exclusion Zone — Life After Fallout

Dark skies and silent streets mark the Chernobyl Exclusion Zone, where disaster paused human life but nature reclaimed its throne. The ghost town and its radioactive forests hold secrets of catastrophe and resilience. Walk the cracked roads and hear the echoes of a world forever changed.

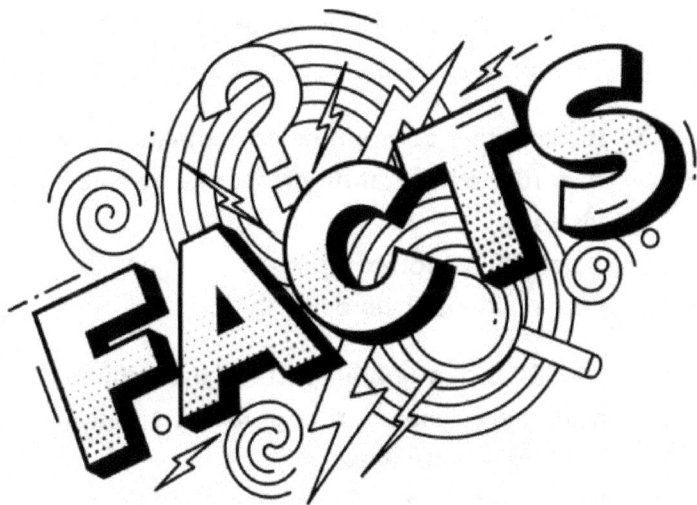

1. **The Chernobyl Exclusion Zone covers about 2,600 square kilometers around the nuclear disaster site.**
   Established after the 1986 reactor explosion, it remains a highly irradiated forbidding region with restricted access.

2. **Radiation levels vary widely, with some hotspots extremely dangerous for humans.**
   Despite this, parts of the zone have seen natural wildlife recovery due to human absence.

3. **The city of Pripyat near the reactor was evacuated within days of the accident.**
   Since then, it has become a ghost town frozen in time—abandoned buildings and belongings left behind.

4. **Flora and fauna have rebounded, creating an unintended wildlife sanctuary.**

Species like wolves, bears, and rare birds have thrived without human disturbance.

5. **Radioactive contamination remains a health hazard, necessitating protective gear for visits.**
   Strict safety protocols govern tours, and long-term residency is forbidden.

6. **UNESCO designated parts of the zone a biosphere reserve, recognizing its unique ecological recovery.**
   It's among the few places where ecosystems evolve post-nuclear disaster.

7. **The sarcophagus enclosing Reactor 4 limits further radiation leaks but is aging.**
   Recent construction of a New Safe Confinement structure enhanced containment measures.

8. **Liquidators and cleanup workers suffered severe health consequences.**
   Their heroic efforts mitigated disaster impact but resulted in extensive exposure to radiation.

9. **The zone attracts scientists studying radiation's effects on biology and ecosystems.**
   Long-term research projects probe mutation rates, species adaptation, and environmental recovery.

10. **Tourism to Chernobyl has grown in recent years, with official guided visits.**

Visitors experience a sobering history lesson combined with glimpses of resilient nature.

11. **Radioactive substances have seeped into soils, water, and food chains.**
Monitoring and remediation efforts continue decades after the disaster.

12. **Evidence of human habitation existed for decades, with some residents defying evacuation.**
Known as "self-settlers," a handful of survivors remain despite government prohibitions.

13. **Abandoned villages and infrastructure provide visual time capsules of Soviet-era life.**
Photographs and film document these haunting, decayed landscapes.

14. **The accident significantly influenced global nuclear safety protocols and policies.**
Legacy lessons have shaped reactor designs and emergency responses worldwide.

15. **Wildlife includes endangered Przewalski's horses successfully reintroduced to the zone.**
These efforts demonstrate attempts to restore historical biodiversity.

16. **Forest fires in recent years have raised radiation remobilization concerns.**
Burnt vegetation releases radioactive particles back into the atmosphere temporarily.

17. **The reactor explosion released massive amounts of radioactive iodine and cesium isotopes.**
These remain key contaminants affecting environmental and human health.

18. **The zone's cleanup and containment have cost billions and require ongoing international cooperation.**
Funding and expertise come from Russia, Ukraine, and global organizations.

19. **Chernobyl inspired multiple documentaries, books, and a popular television series.**
Its historical, scientific, and human tragedy has captivated global attention.

20. **Despite disaster, nature's resilience in the zone offers hope for post-nuclear recovery worldwide.**
Chernobyl exemplifies complex interactions between technology, humanity, and nature.

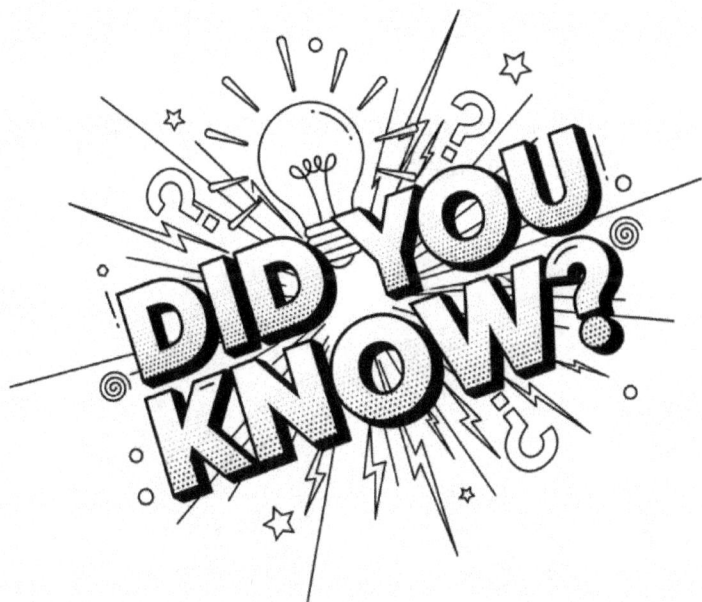

- Pripyat's Ferris wheel remains rusting as a symbol of abandonment.

- Radiation exposure risk halves approximately every seven years (half-life).

- Over 350,000 people were relocated due to contamination.

- Some animals show increased mutation rates, but populations thrive.

- The New Safe Confinement structure weighs 36,000 tons.

- The zone hosts wolves, boars, and over 200 bird species now.

- 'Red Forest' got its name from pine trees killed by radiation.

- Wild mushrooms and berries still pose contamination risks.

19. The Bohemian Grove — Power in the Pines

Every year, a hidden grove in California's redwoods plays host to the powerful and privileged, cloaked in ritual and secrecy. The Bohemian Grove is a retreat unlike any other, where influence is wielded beneath towering trees. Peer beyond the veil of exclusivity and ancient ceremony.

1. **The Bohemian Grove is a private, all-male club and campground in California's redwoods.**
   Owned by the Bohemian Club, it hosts influential figures from politics, business, and arts since 1872.

2. **Each summer, the club gathers for two weeks of private retreats and networking.**
   Exclusive membership includes CEOs, government officials, and top elites.

3. **The Grove is famous for its secrecy and ritualistic ceremonies.**
   Participants engage in theatrical performances, symbolic rites, and informal policymaking discussions.

4. **Guests are sworn to strict confidentiality, with no press allowed.**

This privacy has spawned numerous conspiracy theories about backroom deals.

5. **The 'Cremation of Care' is one of the Grove's signature ceremonies.**
   A theatrical ritual symbolizing release of worldly concerns at the start of the retreat.

6. **Though mythologized, the Grove is primarily a social and networking venue.**
   Its exclusivity nurtures personal relationships among powerful attendees.

7. **Notable past attendees include U.S. presidents, CEOs, and influential artists.**
   These mingle in an environment far removed from public scrutiny.

8. **The Grove covers over 2,700 acres of protected redwood forest.**
   The natural setting offers privacy and solitude for participants.

9. **Security is tight during events, with controlled access and private security.**
   Visitors without invitation are denied entry, enhancing the club's exclusivity.

10. **Discussions at the Grove have influenced policy debates informally.**
    While no official decisions are made, exchanges here can shape opinions and alliances.

11. **Artists and musicians often perform for the members.**

These cultural activities are a tradition within the closed community.

12. **Numerous documentaries and books have attempted to penetrate the Grove's secrecy.**
Their attempts have revealed only glimpses, fueling intrigue and suspicion.

13. **Women were only admitted in guest roles, but gender inclusivity remains controversial.**
Historically, the club has been male-only, sparking modern debates.

14. **Media coverage is severely limited and tightly controlled.**
This enhances the club's aura of exclusivity and discretion.

15. **Members use the retreat for informal diplomacy and business networking.**
Many friendships and alliances, public and private, begin or strengthen at the Grove.

16. **The Grove is private property with extensive conservation efforts for redwoods.**
Environmental stewardship is part of the club's mission in maintaining the grounds.

17. **It has been the focus of various political and conspiracy theories.**
Claims range from secret power brokering to more unfounded speculations.

18. **Bohemian Grove fosters an environment aimed at relaxation away from daily**

pressures.
This atmosphere promotes openness and camaraderie among powerful men.

19. **Innovative ideas and philanthropic projects have reportedly been seeded here.**
The retreat allows for creative thinking in a confidential setting.

20. **Despite its secrecy, the Grove symbolizes elite social and political networks in America.**
It is a microcosm of influence where personal and public power intersect.

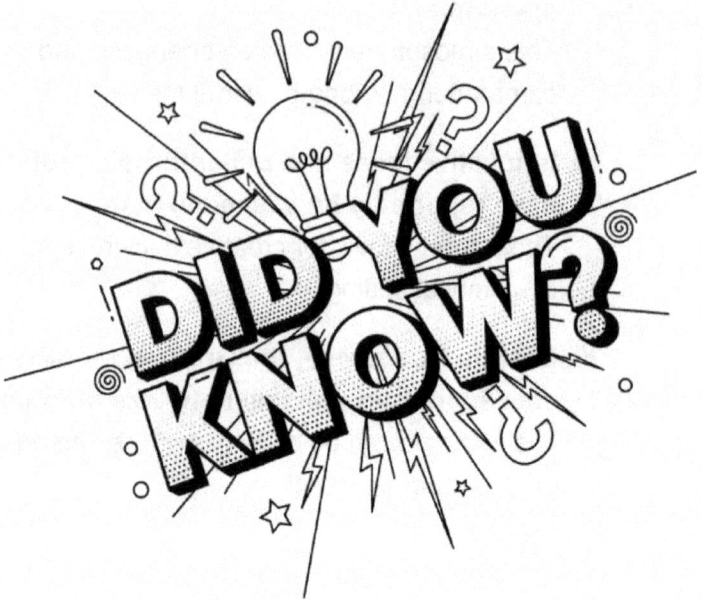

- The 'Cremation of Care' involves a large owl statue symbolizing wisdom.

- Bohemian Grove has been called "the summer camp for the super-rich."

- Membership reportedly costs tens of thousands of dollars annually.

- U.S. presidents from Herbert Hoover onward have attended.

- The Grove hosts various artistic and theatrical events.

- Many business deals start through connections made here.

- Secluded location and natural setting cover 2,700+ acres.

- Several documentaries have attempted to uncover its secrets.

20. Lascaux Cave — France's Frozen Prehistory

Hidden underground in France, Lascaux Cave shelters paintings etched by hands long vanished, speaking volumes across millennia. These ancient images shine a light on early humanity's artistic soul and spiritual journey. Descend into the shadows of prehistory and witness the birth of creativity.

1. **Lascaux Cave contains one of the most famous collections of prehistoric cave paintings.**
   Discovered in 1940, its Paleolithic art dates back approximately 17,000 years.

2. **The cave paintings depict animals such as horses, deer, and bison in vivid detail.**
   These images provide insight into Ice Age human life and spirituality.

3. **Access to the original cave was closed to the public in 1963 to prevent damage.**
   Human presence had led to unstable air quality harming the delicate pigments.

4. **Replicas of Lascaux's chambers have been constructed for public viewing.**
   These simulate the cave environment and preserve the original site.

5. **The paintings exhibit advanced techniques including shading and perspective.**
   They demonstrate early humans' artistic skill and symbolic thinking.

6. **Archaeologists use non-invasive methods to study the cave and its art.**
   Technologies like laser scanning help monitor and preserve the paintings.

7. **The cave's exact purpose remains debated—art, ritual, or communication.**
   Many theories exist about why Ice Age humans created such detailed imagery.

8. **Lascaux is part of the UNESCO World Heritage-listed Vézère Valley.**
   It's acknowledged globally as a key site of prehistoric cultural heritage.

9. **Microbial growth, partially from human visitation, threatened the cave's paintings.**
   Efforts to combat fungus include limiting access and controlling airflows.

10. **The cave's geology includes limestone formations that preserved the paintings.**
    Stable conditions inside the cave helped safeguard the art for millennia.

11. **Stone tools and artifacts found nearby link the cave to early human occupation.**
    These findings complement the artistic evidence in reconstructing prehistoric life.

12. **The cave's art influenced modern appreciation of prehistoric culture and art history.**
It represents one of the richest sources of knowledge about Ice Age societies.

13. **Lascaux's paintings display multiple layers, some dating from different periods.**
This suggests repeated use or reworking over centuries.

14. **Many paintings emphasize animals considered vital to hunter-gatherer survival.**
They highlight the relationship between humans and nature.

15. **The cave also contains abstract signs and symbols whose meanings remain unclear.**
These may represent early forms of communication or spirituality.

16. **Scientific dating techniques, including radiocarbon methods, helped establish the cave's age.**
Advances in archaeology continue refining timelines for prehistoric art.

17. **Restored fragments and artworks are displayed in regional museums near the cave.**
These support educational and cultural tourism while protecting originals.

18. **The cave's discovery sparked a surge in Paleolithic interest and research.**

It broadened understanding of early human cognition and culture.

19. **Similar caves across Europe confirm widespread prehistoric artistic activity.**
Lascaux stands out for its scale, preservation, and artistic quality.

20. **The site illustrates how ancient humans perceived and interacted with their environment.**
It connects modern society with the origins of human creativity.

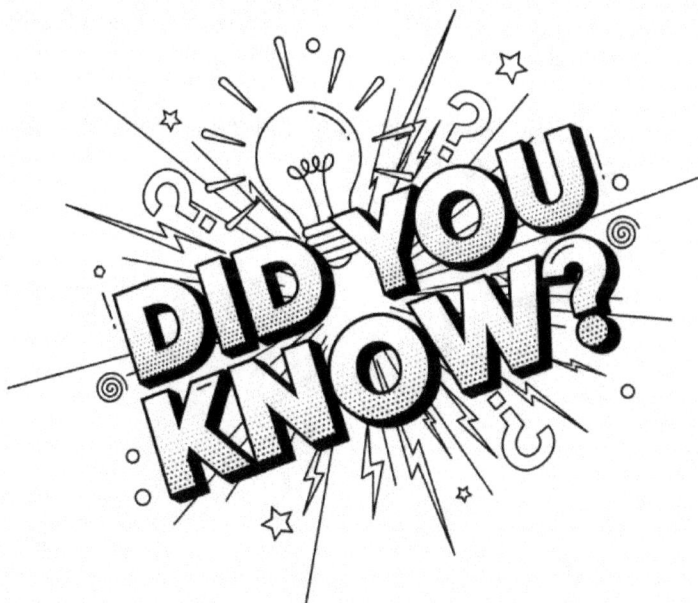

DID YOU KNOW?

- Lascaux Cave contains over 600 animals depicted in its paintings.

- The original cave was sealed naturally many thousands of years ago.

- Flames used by prehistoric painters left charcoal remains studied today.

- Some paintings show evidence of early use of perspective.

- The cave's high humidity complicates preservation efforts.

- Lascaux's replica, Lascaux II, was created to preserve the originals.

- Prehistoric artists used natural mineral pigments like ochre and charcoal.

- The cave inspired global awareness of human prehistoric artistry.

21. Diego Garcia — The Island That Vanished

In the vast Indian Ocean, Diego Garcia is a fortress of strategic might and silent history. Its native people vanished, replaced by a clandestine military base that commands the seas. Unveil the haunting story of this remote island lost between geopolitics and remembrance.

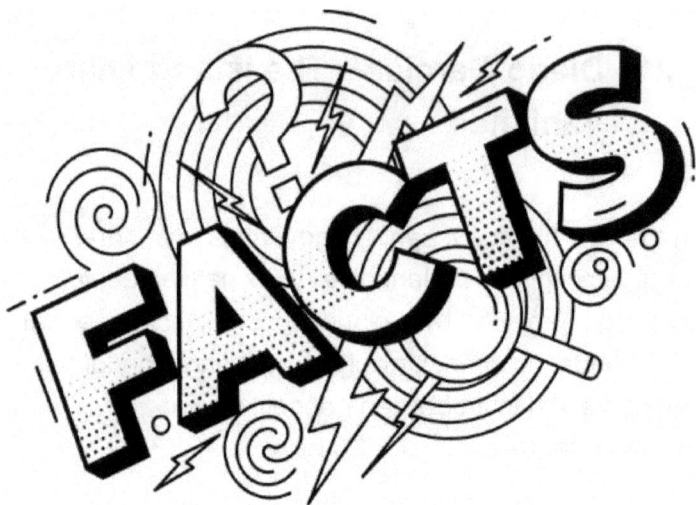

1. **Diego Garcia is a remote atoll in the Indian Ocean, home to a major U.S. military base.**
   It serves as a strategic logistics, surveillance, and defense installation for the U.S. and UK.

2. **The island's native population was forcibly removed between 1968 and 1973.**
   The depopulation was controversial, with former residents demanding resettlement rights.

3. **Diego Garcia's base supports operations across the Middle East and Asia-Pacific regions.**
   It facilitates aerial refueling, naval resupply, and intelligence missions.

4. **The island boasts an expansive airfield capable of handling the largest military aircraft.**

Such capacity makes it essential for strategic rapid deployment.

5. **Its isolated location enhances security but complicates supply and communication.**
   Operations require significant logistics support due to remoteness.

6. **The island's coral reefs and marine life have faced ecological impacts from base activities.**
   Environmental monitoring and mitigation efforts attempt to balance military use and conservation.

7. **Diego Garcia remains a political flashpoint, with Mauritius contesting its sovereignty.**
   International disputes persist regarding the island's legal status.

8. **The base played a major role in the Gulf War, Afghanistan, and Iraq military campaigns.**
   Its strategic position allows rapid engagement in regional conflicts.

9. **Facilities include radar, missile defense systems, and underwater surveillance installations.**
   These provide multi-domain operational capabilities.

10. **The island's infrastructure includes housing, medical facilities, and recreational amenities.**
    It supports a population of thousands of military and civilian personnel.

11. **Diego Garcia's military presence includes cooperation with British forces.**
A joint UK-U.S. effort strengthens shared defense objectives.

12. **The island has no indigenous or permanent civilian population.**
Its use is exclusively military and limited to designated personnel.

13. **Regular patrols and satellite oversight monitor maritime approaches.**
These help secure regional waters against illicit activity.

14. **The base has sparked environmental concerns over waste disposal and habitat disruption.**
Efforts continue to minimize ecological footprint amid operational needs.

15. **Diego Garcia supports strategic communication with submarines and naval vessels.**
This enhances global situational awareness in critical sea lanes.

16. **Its origin is volcanic, with coral atolls surrounding a submerged volcanic cone.**
This unique geology shapes the island's structure and ecosystem.

17. **The island was uninhabited until the mid-20th century when the base was established.**

Prior to that, it had a small British colonial settlement.

18. **Diego Garcia is critical for intelligence collection in the Indian Ocean region.**
Signals interception and reconnaissance platforms operate continuously.

19. **Access is highly restricted due to military sensitivity.**
No tourism or unauthorized visits are allowed.

20. **The base's secrecy fuels speculation and strategic importance globally.**
Its presence underpins U.S. defense posture across several continents.

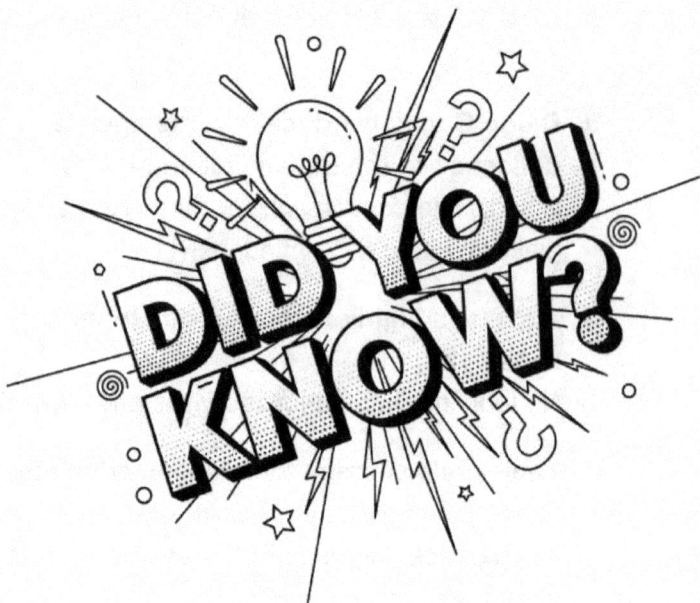

DID YOU KNOW?

- The native Chagossian people seek the right to return to Diego Garcia.

- The airbase can accommodate the C-5 Galaxy, one of the world's largest cargo planes.

- The island is approximately 1,100 miles south of India.

- The U.S. has invested over $1 billion in base upgrades.

- Diego Garcia is key for missile defense systems in the Indian Ocean.

- Coral reefs around the island are biologically rich but vulnerable.

- The island's lagoon is a natural harbor used by naval vessels.

- Its location makes it ideal for monitoring vital shipping routes.

22. Conclusion

The world is full of places hidden in plain sight, locked away by secrecy, geography, or time. Through this collection of 20 extraordinary chapters, we've embarked on a fascinating journey—unveiling the mysteries and realities behind some of the planet's most secretive locations. Each fact and insight has helped illuminate the history, science, and human stories concealed within these guarded spaces.

From the isolated sentinel tribes safeguarding their ancient ways to the clandestine operations of military strongholds; from the preservation of ancient knowledge in Vatican vaults to islands abandoned and reclaimed by nature—these stories remind us how much remains unseen and how curiosity is the key to understanding our world better.

As you close this book, may you carry with you a deeper appreciation for the intricate layers of secrecy protecting powerful, delicate, and sometimes haunting human legacies. The allure of the unknown calls us to explore further, question boldly, and reflect on the balance between secrecy and discovery in shaping our shared history.

May this journey inspire your own quests for knowledge, reminding us all that beyond every locked door and quiet forest lies a story waiting to be told.

www.ingramcontent.com/pod-product-compliance
Lightning Source LLC
LaVergne TN
LVHW051348080426
835509LV00020BA/3344